CHRISTIAN COMMUNICATIONS AND HUMAN RESOURCES

'Dipo Toby Alakija

© Copyright 2016 by Dipo Toby Alakija.

All rights reserved by Calvary Rock Resources. No part of this book may be reproduced or transmitted in any form or by any means without written permission of the publisher through any of the addresses below, apart from the use of short quotations or occasional page copying for personal or group study.

ISBN: 978-073-509-7
ISBN: 978-978-073-509-8

Printed in United States
Published by the publishing house of
CALVARY ROCK RESOURCES
19, Ajina Street, Ikenne Remo,
Ogun State,
Nigeria.

36, Thomson road
Gorton
Manchester
M18 7QQ
United Kingdom

270 Madison Avenue
Suite 1500, New York, NY 10016
United States

www.calvaryrock.org

REAL CHRISTIANS HAVE THE GREATEST OF ALL GIFTS OF GOD

This claim is not an empty or vague statement but the Gospel truth. With the greatest Gift of all gifts of God called the Holy Spirit, Christians can be the living testimonies or witnesses of the passage in Philippians 4:13 which says, *"I can do all things through Christ who strengthens me."* The Spirit of God in a Christian makes him or her far greater, far more powerful, far more knowledgeable, far more skillful and far more intelligent than any other group of people on earth. This is because the Holy Spirit in a Christian makes him or her the son or daughter of ALMIGHTY GOD!

As a child of God, a Christian can operate with the power of God. With the power of God, a Christian has what it takes to become what God destines him or her to be in life in spite of all human limitations. Thus Christians must not let the secular world brainwash them with their comments. They need not allow secular professionalism makes them feel inadequate or inferior to the professionals in the world. It is the devil that discourages Christians, threatening them with failures and making them feel unfit for the work. He makes things look so difficult to accomplish even though God makes them so easy for them through the power of the Holy Spirit. The secular world always make the Christians feel inadequate unless they are trained in the secular ways. While it must be admitted that secular training may be required in some areas, it must be pointed out that most of the things in the secular world are opposed to the gospel.

Christians need to be trained before they can be effective in their ministries but not in the way of the world. The reason lies in the truth that is found in Isaiah 55:8-9, which says, *"For my thoughts are not your thoughts, neither are your ways my ways, saith the LORD. For as the heavens are higher than the earth, so are my ways higher than your ways, and my thoughts than your thoughts."*

Through the above passage Christians know that they do not need to study education in secular way before they can teach the Bible everywhere. They do not need to study communications before they can communicate the word of God effectively to everybody. They do not need to study Child Psychology in school before they can handle or minister to children. They do not need to study music before they can sing songs to the Lord or go into music ministries. They do not need to study Theater Art before they can dramatize the Gospel of

Jesus Christ. The truth is: They are not people of many parts but they have the Holy Spirit inside them who gives them much more than many parts. The Holy Spirit knows all things and can do all things through anyone of who is ready to learn The Word Of God in The Way Of God and by The Will Of God.

Give Holy Spirit the chance to teach you on how you can make exploit for God. Then the passage in Philippians 4:13 will become a reality in your life and the ministries God have called you into.

CHRISTIAN ORAL COMMUNICATIONS

BOOK ONE

INTRODUCTION

Although this course, Christian Oral Communications complements Christian Communication Arts but the basic principle is found in Colossians 3:16-17, which says, *"Let the word of Christ dwell in you richly in all wisdom; teaching and admonishing one another in Psalms and Hymns and spiritual songs, singing with grace in your hearts to the Lord. And whatsoever ye do in word or deed, do all in the name of the Lord Jesus, giving thanks to God and the Father by him."* This passage indicates a few things about Christian Oral Communications but before treating them, the course needs to be defined according to its purpose.

DEFINITION

Using the above passage in Colossians 3:16-17 as the biblical basis of this course, Christian Oral Communications can be defined as ways of ministering, educating or communicating the word or mind of God to one or more persons through spoken words and or the other ways. The passage points out three reasons all Christians need to master the art of oral communications, which may be as follows:

1. With oral communication, they can effectively share the wisdom of God
2. They can teach the word of God and
3. They can admonish one another, encouraging others in righteousness and in right standing with God.

According the same passage, the methodologies of Christian Oral Communications are essentially in two ways which are (i) speaking of the word and (ii) doing the word that is spoken. In essence, for Christians to make any meaningful impact through what they teach or say anywhere, they need to apply in their lives what they teach and say to others.

Speaking Of The Word: Jesus addresses the issues of teaching the word of God without doing it in Matthew 23:3, saying *"All therefore whatsoever they (The Pharisees and Sadducees) bid you observe, that observe and do; but do not ye after their works: for they say, and do not."* There had been eloquent and influential orators who teach others the truth but never apply it in their lives right from the days of Jesus. This group of people which still exits till now has included impostors as part of them. The impostors are the worst set of teachers in this generation. The impostors, according to 2 Timothy 3:5-6, are having a form of godliness, but denying the power thereof. The Bible further warns that other people should turn away from them because, according to verse 6, they creep into house of God and Christian homes either through the media or entertainment, leading people who are once save into captivity.

Doing Of The Word: The Lord further said in Matthew 23:4-7, *"For they (The Pharisees and Sadducees) bind heavy burdens and grievous to be borne, and lay them on men's shoulders; but they themselves will not move them with one of their fingers. But all their works they do for to be seen of men: they make broad their phylacteries, and enlarge the borders of their garments, And love the uppermost rooms at feasts, and the chief seats in the synagogues, And greetings in the markets, and to be called of men, Rabbi, Rabbi."* The word of God makes it clear that Christian Oral Communications is not just communicating or teaching sound principles but also following it to the last letter. Secondly, in other to win the respect of others, many leaders love to teach hard and often times unscriptural principles which they cannot follow. Thus some Christians' doings do not match what they say or teach. Christians who do not practice what they say or teach only make them appear like hypocrites before their students or audiences.

RUDIMENTS OF CHRISTIAN ORAL COMMUNICATIONS

Since there are rules peculiar to each art or act and since Christian Oral Communications involve passing information or knowledge, especially in relation to Christian way of life, it follows that there are rules to be applied. The biblical basis for the law and rudiments is found in Deuteronomy 11:16-20, which says, *'Take heed to yourselves, that your heart be not deceived, and ye turn aside, and serve other gods, and worship them; And then the LORD'S wrath be kindled against you, and he shut up the heaven, that there be no rain, and that the land yield not her fruit; and lest ye perish quickly from off the good land which the LORD giveth you. Therefore shall ye lay up these my words in your heart and in your soul, and bind them for a sign upon your hand, that they may be as frontlets between your eyes. And ye shall teach them your children, speaking of them when thou sittest in thine house, and when thou walkest by the way, when thou liest down, and when thou risest up. And thou shalt write them upon the door posts of thine house, and upon thy gates...'*

The above passage of the scriptures points out that there is need to communicate the messages of God to every category of people, including children; teaching and speaking about them from time to time and from place to place. Since Christian Oral and other forms of Communications in general may not strictly be a two-way communication, the followings can be inferred from the above and other Bible passages as essentials in all:

1. ***KNOWLEDGE OF THE SUBJECT***: This is the first golden rule in all forms of Communications, especially Christian Oral Communication. Since this type Communication is all about educating or communicating to the people the ways of life as designed by God and, just as a teacher who must master the subject he wants to teach, a Christian communicator needs to have the details of the message he wants to pass across to others and master the way to effectively pass it. Without thorough knowledge of the subject to be treated, the communicator would convey the wrong message or information. The more knowledge a Christian communicator has in the Bible, which is the central of the lesson or information in Christian communications, the more he can authoritatively communicate the word and the mind of God. The more gifted a Christian communicator who has little or no knowledge of the Bible, the easier it is for him to go into heresies or mislead the audience.

2. ***UNDERSTAND THE ASSIMILATION CAPACITY OF YOUR AUDIENCE***: **This is another golden rule that must be followed in both Christian Oral and other Communications. Failure to understand this leads to futility and waste of resources. Jesus said in Matthew 7:6,** *"Give not that which is holy unto the dogs, neither cast ye your pearls before swine, lest they trample them under their feet, and turn again and rend you."* **The passage can be used to suite the purpose of this point if it is interpreted like this,** *"Do not waste your precious time giving spiritual food to those who are not yet save nor give meat to baby Christians who are still comfortable living in sins."* Instead of trying to teach or communicate a sound biblical doctrine to a sinner, lead him to Jesus Christ first with the message of salvation. You may not need to quote the Bible to him because he may not even understand it, let alone believe it. Some years ago, I tried telling a man about the need to be born-again. He told me he already heard the message in the Church several times. He even quoted John 3:3, which made me asked if he was born-again. His answer was straight NO! He claimed to be a Christian but he was

quick to add, *"I am not the fanatical type like you guys."* When I understood his problem, I began to use what he can perceive with his human senses to lead him to Christ. From there, I let him realize how important it is to study the word of God that can make him grow. I never introduce any Church. He responded positively to the message.

3. **REPETITION OF POINTS**: The Bible passages in Deuteronomy 11:16-20 established the fact that repetition is part of education. Thus a Christian communicator must develop the creative way of repeating the points in his lesson. If it is a message, he needs to know how to summarize and repeat it to the audience. This is necessary because messages or lessons that are repeated can be retained in the memory longer than when it is not. Besides if any of the points is missed in the first instance, it would be received when it is repeated. Moreover, most people find it hard to remember details of lessons and messages, especially the ones they find uninteresting or boring. Propagandists use repetition of disinformation to mislead the public.

4. **CLEAR PRESENTATIONS**: This is essential in all manners of communications. Obviously you have not communicated if presentation of message or lesson is not clear. Thus a Christian communicator must not be ambiguous in his presentations. The information must be assessable and clear through (i) language or terms the audience can understand (ii) the tempo of speech which must not be fast or slow and (iii) if the lesson or information to be presented is based on previous knowledge, the communicator must be sure the students or audience already acquired the knowledge either by reviewing the precious lessons or by asking them assessment questions.

5. **SIMPLICITY OF COMMUNICATIONS**: A teacher sometimes teaches a complicated subject in somewhat complicated manner but a communicator goes extra mile to make it as simple as possible. The difference is that a communicator studies two sides of the complicated subject which are (i) he studies and understands the subject thoroughly and (ii) he studies the way to make it simple for the audience to understand. More often than, not a Christian communicator may need to use illustrations and stories to pass the message across just as Jesus Christ used

parables to communicate to the people. Recently, I taught some elderly people in a programme I tagged: "Catch Them Old If You Can't Catch Them Young." Because elderly people do not think fast like young ones and can even fall asleep as you talk with them, I adopted the real life story method of teaching which kept their brains active. I asked them the lessons in the story I shared with them so as to gauge if I have communicated the message. They understood the points beyond the level I expected because somehow the story was very intriguing.

REASONS FOR CHRISTIAN ORAL COMMUNICATIONS

Since Christian Oral Communications often times involve physical appearances, some rules may be distinct from other forms of communications. In 1 Timothy 2:8-11, Paul said, *"I will therefore that men pray everywhere, lifting up holy hands, without wrath and doubting. In like manner also, that women adorn themselves in modest apparel, with shamefacedness and sobriety; not with broided hair, or gold, or pearls, or costly array; But (which becometh women professing godliness) with good works. Let the woman learn in silence with all subjection."* The last verse may sound somewhat controversial but it is not. Paul was telling women who were almost segregated in those days to first learn in silence. Unlike in modern days when they are as educated as men, women by the nature of their position in those days were mostly untutored. So Paul does not want to risk giving room for women who were usually illiterate to teach. Both men and women, according to Joel; 2:28-29, now receive the outpour of the Spirit of God. They can now prophesy and see dreams. The implication of that is to communicate to others the visions or dreams they receive from God. All truly born-again, Spirit filled Christians have the ministries of speaking the mind of God to everybody through one way or the other. At least, they have the duty to inform other people about eternity. Thus there is need for them to develop the art of oral communications. The following reasons further establish the Biblical basis for these needs:

1. The ability to communicate effectively is required if a Christian wants to carry out the specific instruction of Jesus Christ who said to all Christians in Mark 16:15-16, *"Go ye into all the world, and preach the gospel to every creature. He that believeth and is baptized shall be saved; but he that believeth not shall be damned."*
2. In Act 2:40, the Bible says, *"And with many other words did he*

testify and exhort, saying, Save yourselves from this untoward generation." In essence, to use the word of God to exhort or deliver people from problems, sins and eternal damnation; the art of Christian Oral Communications needs to be mastered.

3. In 1Peter 2:2, the Bible says, *"As newborn babes, desire the sincere milk of the word, that ye may grow thereby…"* In order to build babes of Christ into soldiers, the art of communications is required.

4. In Proverb 22:6, the Bible says, **"Train up a child in the way he should go: and when he is old, he will not depart from it."** So to minister the word of God to family members like children, acquaintances or friends and collogues requires the art of Christian oral communications.

DISTINCT RULES OF ORAL COMMUNICATIONS

Following Paul's instruction in 1 Timothy 2:8-11 in relation to teaching the Bible, which forms the basis of the rules, the followings are to be applied to everyone involved in Christian Oral Communications.

DRESSING: According to the injunction above, every Christian must be in modest apparel. Modest apparel is further explains as a proper form of dressing. An adage that says *"your dressing speaks volume of whom you are"* applies here. Also note that dressing in modest apparel is part of godliness. There are so many preachers on the T.V and other places whose dressing tell the audience the kind of spirits inside them. A very reputable Pastor made the mistake of inviting from another country a preacher who has wrong dressing orientation to teach his congregation some years ago. The preacher encouraged shameless dressing in his teaching because to dress almost half naked is not a big deal in his country. When the preacher left, the Pastor has the duty to clean up the "vomit" on the pulpit. He took two oranges to the Church. One was ripe while the other was plain green. He asked the congregation, *"which of these oranges has sweet juice?"* Of course, the people pointed at the ripe orange. He asked, *"how do you know? You have not tasted it."* The people said they could see it from the looks of the ripe orange that it would be sweet while the other one would be sour. Then the Pastor pointed out that he did not need to be told the kind of spirit in a woman who dressed shamelessly.

Jesus said in Matthew 7:16, *"you will know them by their fruits."* Fruits can be seen in works and appearances of the bearer. Do not expect anyone who says one thing but his or her dressing speaking another thing to make much positive impact. A great man of God whose counsel is always regarded as authority in Christendom in Nigeria was asked, "how should a Christian dresses?" He told his wife whose dressing typically portrayed Bible form of dressing to walk round in front of the people. After she did that, he told them, *"that is the way a Christian should dress."* There is another case of a preacher whose wife sometimes preached with him on TV. She dressed in a way that misrepresented genuine Christianity while preaching on TV. In Christian Oral Communications, your dressing is part of the art of communications because it can further inform or misinform your audience or students. Whether you know it or not, whether you believe it or not, audience knows how to class you through your dressing. Some may say of some ministers *"her dressing really shows she is a Christian."* They may say of others, *"She is a fashion model."* Some may say, *"the dress reveal the shape of her body which I love…"* And yet the Bible says Romans14:21, *"It is good neither to eat flesh, nor to drink wine, nor any thing whereby thy brother stumbleth, or is offended, or is made weak."* Unknown to many people, their mode of dressing divert attentions from the ministrations. While you need to be dressed in such a modest and humble manner that portrays Christianity, you must not dress in a shabby or untidy or humiliating or dirty manner. If Jesus was not so neat when he was on earth, the soldiers that crucified him would not divide and cast lots with his garments, according to Matthew 27:32-35. So modesty and neatness of clothing are one of the crucial rules in Christian Oral Communications.

IRRITATING MANNERISM : There are some habits that may not really constitute any sin but are irritating enough to put people off. Recently in my church, I requested a Pastor to pray for a family who came for thanksgiving service with friends. As he prayed, I noticed just before I closed my own eyes in prayer that he held the microphone with one hand and pocketed the other hand. The gesture and other mannerism gave the impression that he was a pompous and self confident. I looked round at the congregation. There were few people looking irritated at the mannerism. This pastor may not be as pompous or proud as he seemed but his mannerism gives the impression. Constant gesticulations or gesture can constitute irritating mannerism. I had that problem at the early stage of my ministries. I almost always wanted to use hands to describe everything I said as if I was addressing deaf people. All actions or gesticulations and gestures must be well composed if at all you need them while teaching. There are other irritating mannerism like picking nose and habitually repeating words which are not necessary at all. Such as saying, *"you know… you see…"*

EXPRESSIONS: These come in different ways like facial expressions, action and even silence. Expressions make impressions. Anymore involved in Christian Oral Communications must be conscious of the way he expresses himself through any way. Apart from the tone of your voice, you can also express yourself through action. You are familiar with the adage that says, *"action speaks louder than voice."* This implies that your action carries more weight than your voice. If you are fond of laughing or smiling, you will provoke laughter or smiles. If you are fond of looking sad, you are likely to provoke sadness. Sad expressions piss people off easily because no one wants to be sad. The same principle is applicable to confident looks. It tells people that you are sure of what you are saying. If you express doubt while communicating any message, your audience or students are not likely to believe or take you seriously. One of the gimmicks of advertisers or marketers uses to persuade people to by their products is their expressions and the aura of confidence. Thus if they hold a blue cup for the audience to see, with high level of confidence and serious expressions, they can make the audience believe the cup is green. That is what expressions can do. Any Christian who believes he is communicating the truth, he or she must say it with confidence and authority because people can easily spot it in your expressions. I remember a time I gave members of my Church Council the impression that I was afraid of the conduct of man who was doing something wrong yet he believed he was doing what is right. Thinking I was afraid of him, the man emphatically defended his misconduct. Then I told everybody that if anyone sees fear in me, it is the fear of what is going to be an overreaction on my part. **"I know if I strike, lots of people would be hurt,"** I said with stern **expressions on my face. "I don't want to hurt anyone, especially people I am supposed to care for."** Everybody including the man got the message and that brought about instant change. If an expression of doubt either on your face or action is spotted, your audience would either doubt what you are saying or doubt if you know what you saying. The facial expressions of Christians must always be pleasant and confident. They must be full of smiles when talking about the heavenly joy. They must be full of concerns, seriousness and even horror when talking about the consequences of a life without Christ.

THE NEEDS IN CHRISTIAN ORAL COMMUNICATIONS

1. **_HOLY SPIRIT_**: Just like in every ministration, Holy Spirit needs to operate in the life and ministries of all Christian communicators, which include all matured Christians, irrespective of your status; family or academic background. There are so many things which we do not know nor understand nor remember when we are involved in any form of ministrations but with the operation of Holy Spirit, it would look as if we know it all. In Luke 12:11-12, Jesus said, **"And when they bring you unto the synagogues, and unto magistrates, and powers, take ye no thought how or what thing ye shall answer, or what ye shall say. For the Holy Ghost shall teach you in the same hour what ye ought to say."** Without Holy Spirit operating in the life of a Christian, he or she would be using head knowledge to deliver lectures or messages. Head knowledge is much more of academic stuff than spiritual materials. The Bible says in Romans 15: 16-17, **"That I should be the minister of Jesus Christ to the Gentiles, ministering the gospel of God, that the offering up of the Gentiles might be acceptable, being sanctified by the Holy Ghost. I have therefore whereof I may glory through Jesus Christ in those things which pertain to God."** The works of Holy Spirit in the life of a minister cannot be over emphasized. Hence the followings are reasons Christian Oral Communications requires operation of the Holy Spirit in their lives and ministries.

(A) Holy Spirit reveals the mind of God to people through the speaker. So it is not the prophets alone that know the mind of God but as many that are filled with the Holy Spirit. The Bible said in Mark 4:11, **"And he (Jesus) said unto them, 'Unto you it is given to know the mystery of the kingdom of God: but unto them that are without, all these things are done in parables.'"**

(B) Holy Spirit uses the speaker or minister to interpret the word of God accurately to the people. 1 Corinthians 1:18, the Bible says, **"For the preaching of the cross is to them that perish foolishness; but unto us which are saved it is the power of God."** One preacher was leaving the hall where he just finished preaching. As he was outside, holding his Bible, a man approached him and said, *"I admire your conviction and your sincerity when you preached in the hall but I have to tell you that the whole gospel is pure nonsense."*

The preacher opened his Bible and said, *"you're quiet right, you know. The word of God says exactly what you just said now."*

"You're joking, right? The Bible can't possibly say that the gospel is nonsense," the man replied.

The preacher opened to 1 Corinthians 1:18 and read the place to him, *"For the message of the cross is foolishness to those who are perishing, but to us who are saved it is the power of God."*

The preacher closed his Bible and began to leave after establishing his point.

The man recognized it at once that the word of God sounded foolish to him because he was about to perish. He got hold of the preacher and requested him to tell him more. He became born again that day and then, from there, the word of God became the power of God to him. You can note the dramatic method, which through the Holy Spirit, preacher was able to apply the word of God to the argumentative unbeliever.

(C) Holy Spirit convicts the hearer of the word of God. The Bible says in Act 28:27, *"For the heart of this people is waxed gross, and their ears are dull of hearing, and their eyes have they closed; lest they should see with their eyes, and hear with their ears, and understand with their heart, and should be converted, and I should heal them."*

(D) Holy Spirit gives the speaker or minister the strength to make exploit for Christ. Act 1:8 *"But ye shall receive power, after that the Holy Ghost is come upon you: and ye shall be witnesses unto me both in Jerusalem, and in all Judea, and in Samaria, and unto the uttermost part of the earth."*

(E) Holy Spirit helps the speaker or the minister to live by the word of God, leading and helping him or her out of temptation. 1 Corinthians 10:13, the Bible says *"There hath no temptation taken you but such as is common to man: but God is faithful, who will not suffer you to be tempted above that ye are able; but will with the temptation also make a way to escape, that ye may be able to bear it."*

(F) It is only through operation of Holy Spirit that everybody can overcome lust of the flesh and exhibit the fruits of the Spirit that are listed in Galatian5:22-23.

Every Christian is called to shared the word of God, going by the passage in Mrak16:15, Thus we all need Holy Spirit to operate in our lives before we can make any impact in the lives of others.

2. **<u>THE WORD OF GOD</u>**. Jesus commanded all Christians in the passage Mark 16:15, which says, *"And he (Jesus) said unto them (the Christians), 'Go ye into all the world, and preach the gospel to every creature.'"* Since we have to preach to all categories of people in all walks of life, all Christians must be well equipped with the word of God. The more you are equipped with the word, the more the Holy Spirit will use you to teach others. In Psalm 119:104-105, the Bible says, *"Through thy precepts I get understanding: therefore I hate every false way. Thy word is a lamp unto my feet, and a light unto my path."* This passage proves that the word of God is the lamp that lights the path of a Christian life and the ministries. It also indicates that anyone with the word of God is a light or touch bearer. The study of the parable of ten virgins in Matthew 25:1-13 will reveal the importance of the word of God. In that parable, the two categories of virgins represent the two categories of Christians. The five virgins who have extra oil for their lamps represent Christians who are well grounded in the word of God while the rest of the five are not. The five foolish virgins rely on others to equip them with the word of God instead of searching the scriptures by themselves as the passage in John 5:39 says. Jesus said in the passage, *"Search the scriptures; for in them ye think ye have eternal life: and they are they which testify of me."* While waiting for the second coming of Jesus Christ who is represented by the bridegroom, the foolish virgins run out of the word of God (extra oil) that will keep them burning for Christ. They go into the world with the thoughts that they are still in the fold of Christ, seeking for other knowledge. When the Lord comes the second time to take home Christians that are waiting, they are left behind. Any Christian who does not constantly take the word of God would soon find himself going astray. To keep waiting for the Lord, all Christians need the word of God in their lives. This will keep them burning for Christ without running out of oil (the word) in their lamps (lives).

3. **<u>DISCIPLINE</u>**: This is required in almost everything a Christian wants to do for himself or accomplish for the Lord. Lack of discipline turns a Christian into bread and butter believers. In Romans 14:17-21 the Bible says, *"For the kingdom of God is not meat and drink; but*

righteousness, and peace, and joy in the Holy Ghost. For he that in these things serveth Christ is acceptable to God, and approved of men. Let us therefore follow after the things which make for peace, and things wherewith one may edify another. For meat destroy not the work of God. All things indeed are pure; but it is evil for that man who eateth with offence. It is good neither to eat flesh, nor to drink wine, nor any thing whereby thy brother stumbleth, or is offended, or is made weak." The passage indicates that the act of indiscipline of a matured Christian who is seen as a role model can communicate wrong message, making others weak or to stumble. A young lady approached a friend of mine who used reading glasses after preaching in the Church one day and said, *"Pastor, your message is always powerful. When you put on these glasses, you always look so handsome."* When my friend asked her the area of her life that was touched by the message, she has nothing much to say except that it was a powerful message. Then my friend took the glasses and broke it. The lady looked stunned. He told her, *"if my glasses would stand on your way of eternal life, I will sacrifice it. I would ask God to make it possible for me to read without glasses."* My friend passed a vital message to her and everybody that was around. Through discipline, he was able focus on the message and the audience without getting swayed by comments that centre on him as a person. The same act of indiscipline is what makes a Christian compares himself with non-Christian. Like someone rightly pointed out, any Christian who compares himself with non-Christian has made himself unbeliever already. Another person commented that it is not easy to lead soul to Christ. How true! Jesus said in Matthew 11:12, *"And from the days of John the Baptist until now the kingdom of heaven suffereth violence, and the violent take it by force."* If it takes spiritual violence for a person to make heaven, it will take a greater spiritual force to help others to get to heaven. Christians who really have heaven in their hearts must be disciplined in every area of the lives, including eating habits. The body has to be denied of certain things before a Christian can be a blessing to himself and other people. Sometimes, as Paul was trying to teach it in Romans 14:17-20, the speaker or minister will need to deny himself basic things like food and water before he or she can receive from the sprit realm. Sometimes he may need to deny himself of sleep or leisure hour. More often than not, Christian communicators would need to study hard before they can deliver edifying lectures. In all cases of ministrations, there are sacrifices to be made by the minister before anyone can really be blessed by God. It takes discipline before the minister can make such sacrifices.

4. *FAITH*: Everything in Christian life requires in certain things. The Bible describes faith in Hebrew 11:1, *"Now faith is the substance of things hoped for, the evidence of things not seen."* In Christian Oral Communications, the following kinds of faith are required to make impact in the lives of others:

I. ***Faith In God:*** makes it easy to tap into the realm of the spirit and get revelations from God. There was once a highly anointed minister who was involved in healing and word ministries. Two sisters who have heard about him decided to take their seriously sick brother from the hospital to his crusade. They got some men to put him on a stretcher and took him to the front of the minister, telling them, **"be gentle and careful with him."** When they put the sick man in front of the minister, typical of his type of ministrations, he slapped "the devil" that caused the sickness out of him. The sick man fainted. One of his sisters screamed, *"you've killed him! Get the police!"* When the sick man was taken back to the hospital, it was discovered that he was healed. Faith in God makes a Christian operate with divine power. Without faith in God, God cannot be involved in the operations because the Bible says in verse 6 of the same passage in Hebrew, **"But without faith it is impossible to please him: for he that cometh to God must believe that he is, and that he is a rewarder of them that diligently seek him."** Faith in God gives all believers the boldness and confidence to stand before people and minister to them, knowing fully that Jesus will not let the minister down.

II. ***Faith In Christian Ability:*** If a Christian believe and apply the word of God, especially the one in John 1:12 which says, **"But as many as received him, to them gave he power to become the sons of God, even to them that believe on his name,"** He would know that he has the ability of God build inside him. When a person is conscious of the fact that he is a child or servant of God, he will not excise doubt in the ability or power God has given him to operate. Just as Paul said in Philippians 4:13, **"I can do all things through Christ which strengthens me,"** he will say to himself, **"I can teach or talk to these people, however learned or intelligent because I've got my ability from God inside me!"** Do you have what it takes to make them listen even if they do not want to listen? Oh, yes, you do! Consider the case of Peter, a rustic fisherman who was made one of the greatest apostle of Jesus Christ. If God can use someone like that to preach a powerful sermon in the book of Acts 2:14-37 and pricked thousands of people in their hearts, then God can use you. He is always ready to use willing and obedient people. If you have faith in yourself as a child of God, you will be conscious that ministering to people is not about you but about God. Because of that, God will back you up and glorify Himself. Have you ever seen a teenager addressing people who are old enough to be his grand parents, telling them what they do not know despite their age differences? I saw one on a video. In fact the boy who said Jesus revealed to him all he told the people taught me so many things I could not discover in the Bible.

III. **Faith In What You Are Doing:** When you know you are doing things in the name of Lord, Jesus will see to it that you get the desired result. In Colossians 3:17, the Bible says, ***"And whatsoever ye do in word or deed, do all in the name of the Lord Jesus, giving thanks to God and the Father by him."*** You may not get immediate result but certainly you will get the result that will glorify the Name of the Lord. Christians cannot afford to permit discouragement in their lives or ministries. As someone rightly said, God does not use discouraged servant. Faith in what you are doing makes you zealous in making exploits for the Lord. I remember when I started my writing career in early 1980s, the time I was in secondary school. Despite not getting encouragement from anymore, I kept writing. I wrote junks, stories, articles - name it. The only people that encouraged me back then were my friends who were always ready to read whatever junk I wrote even if they did not make much sense to them. The more I wrote, the more I improved. When I got to the point I considered myself a professional writer who deserved to be published, I sent my manuscripts to so many Nigerian publishers who found it easy to note that I was an amateur. I was constantly turned down. I did not get published until I gave my life to Christ. Even then, God still has to train me with the use of the Bible before I was first published by one of the few Nigerian national newspapers known as Sunday Tribune in 1995. In less than 10 years after becoming a columnist, my works find their way to the international market. You must have faith in what you are doing otherwise, no matter who encourages you, you will not go far before you give up. When you have faith in what you are doing, criticism even it is meant to crush you will build you instead of crushing you. Faith in what you are doing is very crucial in Christian Oral Communications.

IV. ***Constant Practice***: To be effective in communication, you need to begin to talk to yourself in front of a mirror. Through that you can easily correct yourself when you make mistakes. You can graduate from there to talking to your friends, asking them what you are missing. You need to listen to their criticism because no matter what they say, they represent a class of people that would feel the same way among your audience. Tell them to find out your mannerism and flaws in your art of communication, asking for scores in the area of effective communication. As pointed out earlier on, you must master the topic you want to treat in line with the word of God. As you constantly practice, you will discover that you are improving on a constant basis.

Christian Oral Communications involve studies and practical experiences. So all Christian communicators must be conversant with the word of God and the topic they want to treat before they face the audience. In a situation where you need to use a text book, you need to study it.

In Christian Oral Communications, stories or illustrations that are relevant to the topics or the subjects may be taken from the Bible or extracted from real life testimonies. The reason is that they add colour to the message and can establish good points if well utilized. However, as good as they may be, they should not be allowed to over shallow the entire subject by taking time to relate them. Any story to be used to establish any point must be very brief. Since Christian Oral Communications is mostly practical, your performance can be best assessed as you deliver your paper or after your talk. Roughly, this is an outline of what a good presentation in Christian Oral Communications entails.

(1) Introduction Of The Topic: After a brief prayer unless it is a prayer meeting, you can introduce the topic in the presentation by:
- (a) If you have a good story or edifying joke to share, you have only three minutes to do that. The story must be very relevant or must lead to the subject. It can be real life experience or Bible story or your personal experience or
- (b) You can sing a song or a hymn hat is also relevant to the subject. This will carry the people along and also motivate them

to listen to you or

(c) You can also begin to quote a passage in the Bible that suggest the subject or a quote of wise saying that may introduce and analysis the subject in line with the Bible. This can also motivate the people to hear you.

(2) The Lecture: There are various methods that can be used, depending on the category of people you are dealing. There are teaching, expository and other methods that can be used. You may need to study Christian Education Methodology or Homiletics to get more information, especially if you are just getting familiar with how to impact knowledge. In the case of children, you may not be able to get all their attentions if you are not good at telling stories. This is the major reason stories are used to teach Christian moral lessons in Calvary Rock Resource children books.

(3) The Conclusion: This is next vital aspect after your presentation. The followings make it vital:
   (a) Since it is difficult for the audience to recall the details, the summaries are always embedded in conclusion of good presentations.
   (b) The conclusion of a presentation points to the audience the lessons so far and
   (c) leads the people to take action or determine what steps that are expected of them, creating rooms for prayers.

Please, understand that when delivering lecture to adults, you may not be required to share stories or jokes, especially if the subject does not create room for that. Secondly, you may categorize the sub-heading of the topic of the subject with various points under each subheadings. Take a look at a sketch of a lecture I delivered at Bible school seminar.

TOPIC: THE SPIRIT OF ERRORS AND THE SPIRIT OF TRUTH

INTRODUCTION: Story of a young man who attended a Church where a preacher says, *"there is hell."* The boy told himself, ***"I don't have to listen to this man. If it is true that there is no hell, then my sins have no grievous consequences. So I can sin as I like because there will be no repercussion. But if his preacher is not telling the truth and I believe him, he will mislead me and I***

will end up in hell!"

MAIN BODY OF THE LECTURE:

A. TYPES OF SPIRITS
1. Unseen Being called Holy Spirit (Acts 1:8, Hebrew 9:8)
2. Unseen part of man that links the soul and body together called human spirit (1 Corinthians 5:3-4, Ecclesiastes 12:7)
3. Unseen beings called evil spirits or demons (Act 19:13-17)

B. WHAT IS ERROR?
1. Ignorance of the word or the way of God (Matthew 22:29, Isaiah 35:6, Hebrew 3:10)
2. Ignorance of Truth (Psalm 25:5-10, Lev. 4:2-13, Hosea 4:6)
3. Heresy of the devil (2 Peter 2:1-3)

C. WHAT IS TRUTH?
1. The word of God is Truth (John 17:17)
2. Jesus is the Truth (John 14:6)
3. The Holy Spirit is Spirit of Truth (John 16:13)

CONCLUSION

The Holy Spirit who is the Spirit of Truth is to teach all Christians. They need to know about their physical, spiritual and eternal lives. Without the word of God, they are vulnerable to the spirit of error which is characterized by demons. These spirit deceive, manipulate and mislead the people with the sole aim of stealing the physical lives of people, using them to commit sins, killing spiritually by separating them from God and the destroying them in hell as pointed in John 10:10. To avoid being separated from God spiritually and eternally, a person must be born-again by giving his or her life to Jesus, develop personal relationship with God, study and then strictly abide by the word of God - the Bible. Shall we pray?

The above outline is not detailed, of course but it is the framework of the presentation, which took about one and a half hours to deliver at the Bible College. It can be more elaborate than that, depending on the teaching grace of the teacher. Outline in this category must always be sketched in a simple way so that it can fit into the time frame that is provided for the speaker. If it is made simple like this, it would serve as guidance on the points that cannot be compromised, giving the audience rooms to joint down vital points. Another reason you can use this type of sketch is because it is flexible. The flexibility makes presentations adaptable to the length of time.

Having explaining the basics of Christian Oral Communications, you can now prepare your paper for presentations using the topic given to you.

Assessment Questions
1. Use passages in the Bible, explain the definition and the basis of Christian Oral Communications.
2. What are the rudiments of Christian Oral Communications?
3. Explain the reasons for Christian Oral Communications.
4. What are the distinct rules of Christian Oral Communications?
5. Holy Spirit and the word of God are vital Christian Oral Communications. Explain.
6. A Christian communicator must be discipline and be full of faith. Explain the reasons.
7. Prepare a paper for presentation to a group of people who need to be convinced of their sins

CHRISTIAN DRAMA COMMUNICATIONS

BOOK TWO

INTRODUCTION

A missionary team went to a village with the hope to lead the villagers to Christ and establish a place of worship for them. All the team members decided to act the story of Jesus as in the Bible. They went round the village, telling the people to come and watch a drama that would transform their lives. Before long, most of the villagers, including children gathered at the centre of the village to watch. Even though most if not all the missionary team members were acting for the first time, the Spirit of God directed all of them, including the ones that acted as Jesus, His disciples, the Sadducees, Pharisees and those who eventually nailed Christ on the cross. When Jesus was crucified, died and buried for the offence He knew nothing about in the drama, the whole villagers, including the head were so moved emotionally that most of them began to cry. When, however, Jesus rouse up on the third day in the drama, the whole village went wild with excitements, attracting the rest of the villagers that were not around at the drama presentation venue. When the drama ministration was concluded, the entire villagers decided to become Christians.

You need to note in the above case that the missionary team members were not dramatist or professionals in drama presentations. There are Christians who simply preached Jesus to the people through Christian Drama Communications and they got a remarkable result that gives a host of heaven joy, going by what the Jesus said in Luke15:7. The passage says, *"I say unto you, that likewise joy shall be in heaven over one sinner that repenteth, more than over ninety and nine just persons, which need no repentance."*

Christians who communicate the word of God through drama are regarded as Drama ministers. Drama ministers are just like other ministers communicate or preach or teach the word of God. In a simple manner, we are going to study Christian Drama Communications as a course and the basic ingredients.

Definition Of Christian Drama Communications: The course is not concerned about literary or academic but biblical definition. Thus the study is strictly going to be within the confine of the Bible.

In Act 21:11-12, the Bible says, *"And when he was come unto us, he took Paul's girdle, and bound his own hands and feet, and said, Thus saith the Holy Ghost, So shall the Jews at Jerusalem bind the man that owneth this girdle, and shall deliver him into the hands of the Gentiles. And when we heard these things, both we, and they of that place, besought him not to go up to Jerusalem."*

According to the above passage, a prophecy which later came to pass was dramatized by a prophet while trying to explain what would happen to Paul. Thus we can say drama ministration is an act of demonstrating the Gospel truth just as we see it in the above passage and in story about the missionary team.

In Luke 10:23, the Bible says, **"And He (Jesus) turned him unto His disciples, and said privately, Blessed are the eyes which see the things that ye see…"**

From this passage, we can say Christian Drama Communications is also a way of improvisations for things that are not readily available for people to see with their eyes. By creating scenes, roles and performances that reveal the truths for them to watch, Christian Drama Communications put into action the mind of God, what has happened or what would happen. You can consider the case of the movie titled: "Passion Of Christ" which brought to life, the life of Jesus Christ as it is recorded in the Bible thousands of years ago. The number of souls that were saved through this movie cannot be determined by anyone. Why is it so? Does it mean people do not read the Bible or preachers do not preach the word of God? No. The truth lies in the adage that says, "seeing is believing." It is little wonder that the devil is using dramas to deceive people. Life itself is a drama called real life drama while the one that are staged is called fake life drama as in the secular. Some movies indicate it at beginning if the story is based on real life story. Christian Drama Communications that conform with the Bible can be regarded as Christian or eternal life drama.

In Colossians 2:15, the Bible says, **"And having spoiled principalities and powers, He (Jesus through Christians) made a show of them openly, triumphing over them in it."**

We also see Christian Drama Communications, according to that passage as a way of making public show through display of what happens in the spirit realm with the use of drama for people to see, giving God the glory and honour.

Christian Drama Communications can thus be defined as act of demonstrating the truth through creations of scenes; roles and performances, making public show of what happens in the spirit realm with sole aim of preaching the truth and to glorify the name of the Lord.

CHARACTERISTICS OF TRUE CHRISTIAN DRAMA COMMUNICATIONS

So many people, especially youths have gone into Christian Drama Communications for the wrong reasons or motives. Many people are deceived or made to believe that they are going into drama ministry to preach the gospel or to glorify the Name of the Lord but the truth is: they do it for self promotion or self glory or to prove that they are good or gifted in acting. In 1 Corinthians 4:4-5 the Bible says, *"For I know nothing by myself; yet am I not hereby justified: but he that judgeth me is the Lord. Therefore judge nothing before the time, until the Lord come, who both will bring to light the hidden things of darkness, and will make manifest the counsels of the hearts: and then shall every man have praise of God."*

In the above passage, it is clear that nobody is justified by the success of his or her doings, including drama and other ministries but justified by the motives behind the doings. It also indicates that no one is in the position to judge the other but the Lord will bring to light the hidden motives of the doings of everyone. In other words, it is your motive in the work of the Lord that will be judged, not the works. In 1 Samuel 16:7, the Bible says, *"But the LORD said unto Samuel, Look not on his countenance, or on the height of his stature; because I have refused him: for the LORD seeth not as man seeth; for man looketh on the outward appearance, but the LORD looketh on the heart."* We can see in this passage that man looks at outward appearance but the Lord looks at the heart.

GOOD MESSAGE/GOODNEWS: A true Christian Drama Communication must always be concerned about preaching the Gospel for the purpose of leading souls to Christ or for the edification of Body of Christ. These are the ultimate reasons for going into drama ministry in the first place. A lot of so-called drama ministers are concerned mainly about the entertainment without putting into considerations the message in the Christian Drama Communications. It is true that there is need for the ministrations to be exciting or entertaining so as to carry the audience along but that must not be done at the expense of the message. If there is misplacement of priorities in Christian Drama Communications like putting the entertainment first, the message would be watered down. Besides, the presentations of the drama may not be different from that of the secular drama. It is therefore instructive to note that the message is the ultimate and it must not be compromised in true Christian Drama

Communications.

Another thing to note here is that the message must be balanced. In other words, it must conform with the scriptures. A lot of drama ministers preach things that are unscriptural, if not heretical. The easiest way to preach heresy is through drama. Unlike on the pulpit while preaching, the preacher would need to refer to the Bible to establish his points, Christian Drama Communications may not need to do that. More often than not, a lot of drama ministers so much entertain or work on the emotion of the people to the extent that they completely stray from the word of God. I have watched several Christian movies that make me feel ashamed of their ministrations. A lot of script writers based their stories on emotions or dreams or events that are manipulated by the devil instead of basing them on the word of God. In 2 Peter 2:1-4, the Bible says, ***"But there were false prophets also among the people, even as there shall be false teachers among you, who privily shall bring in damnable heresies, even denying the Lord that bought them, and bring upon themselves swift destruction. And many shall follow their pernicious ways; by reason of whom the way of truth shall be evil spoken of. And through covetousness shall they with feigned words make merchandise of you: whose judgment now of a long time lingereth not, and their damnation slumbereth not. For if God spared not the angels that sinned, but cast them down to hell, and delivered them into chains of darkness, to be reserved unto judgment..."***

We can see it from this passage that there also false drama ministers who think they are serving God but actually misleading people through the destructive heresies in their drama presentations. The Bible says in that passage that their end is destruction. You can see why a script writer must be called and inspired to write story for Christian Drama Communications. It is not enough for someone to be skillful in script writing. The scriptwriter must also be well grounded in the Bible. The reason is that an heresy can lead to a whole lot of destruction. Some drama ministries do not produce movies based on the scripts that are written by other people outside their ministries, no matter how good. We do not have to blame them because their reasons are best known to them.

<u>PRESENTATIONS:</u> One of the hallmarks that characterizes true Christian Drama Communications are the presentations. Presentations of drama can be explained as the total attributes and manners by which all the roles are interpreted. The way a Christian drama is presented is always different from that of the secular world. In presentation of Christian drama, care is always taken not to divert the minds of the audience from the story to the act. In essence, there are some things or actions that are not fit or permitted in Christian Drama Communications though they may be permitted in secular drama. Since a Christian drama is more of preaching than entertainment, utmost modesty is required in the presentations. In Titus 2:11-14, the Bible says, *"For the grace of God that bringeth salvation hath appeared to all men, Teaching us that, denying ungodliness and worldly lusts, we should live soberly, righteously, and godly, in this present world..."*

Let us itemize few things in Christian drama presentations from the above passage.

i. Through presentations of stage drama or film show, the grace of God that brings about salvation appeared to all men (verse 11).

ii. Christian Drama Communications teach of the need to deny ungodliness and worldly lust instead of encouraging them (ver12). In other words, ungodliness and lusts must never be celebrated or allowed through obscene scenes. For instance, a lot of so-called drama ministers go as far creating lustful scenes just to convince the audience that this is for real. In the cause of doing that, they excite the audience sexually. The case is like a man trying remove a snail from its shell by breaking it. True Christian Drama Communications must not go that far. The audience is not foolish. It is enough to show what goes on if a man and a woman enter a bedroom together, locked the door and lie on the bed together. The audience will get the message. Going as far as removing their cloths, leaving only under wears or caressing each other is going too far. If that is done the Christian Drama Communications will amount to suggestive ministrations, which will amount to anti-Gospel message. The audience may crave for excitements in the suggestive scenes but do not fall into the temptation of creating it because it will destroy the entire ministrations.

iii. As Christian Drama Communication goes on, the audience should be convinced that the ministers live soberly. They should not create scenes that suggest that lustful things is going on behind the scenes. The secular adage says: *"Justice must not only be done but must be seen to have been done."* In other words, Christian dramatists must live soberly, righteously, godly and also must be seen that they live according to what they preach or teach through their Christian Drama Communications.

Having treated a few characteristics of true Christian Drama Communications as much as we can, let us look at the person of a true drama minister.

MOTIVES AND CALLINGS OF A TRUE DRAMA MINISTER

MOTIVES: Since the Lord looks at the heart, our motives and intentions in anything we want to do for the Lord must be pure and holy. If this is absent, the drama minister is at great risks.

I remember a secular dramatist who staged a play to a large audience in one town that is notable for demonic activities a few years ago. This dramatist used some incantations to conjure some demonic beings in the play. The fake demonic beings were below the stage, ready to jump on the platform as soon as the incarnations were over. But before the dramatist completed them, real demonic beings had appeared on the stage, causing panic in the entire place. Everybody, including all the artists took to their heels. The demonic beings were so offended that they marked the dramatist. He repeated the same thing in another town where he was killed on the spot. Now the question is: would he have gone away with it if he had been a true Christian? The answer can be yes and no, depending on his motives and a few other things.

Pure and holy motives are very essential in true Christian Drama Communications.

CALLINGS: Another important characteristic of true Drama minister is calling. Unknown to many people, just because you are gifted does not mean you are called into Christian Drama Communications though you can play a supportive roles, hiding under the calling of the leader of the ministries.

Just like every other ministries, you must be called into drama ministry before you can go away with a lot of things. If you are called to do any work for the Lord, you need to understand the boundary of your ministries. As there are various things involved in Christian Drama Communications, ranging from script writing, directing, interpretations of roles and the like which would be treated later on, you must not work outside your calling. The reason is that your calling would be challenged either by the devil or by people whether you like it or not. It is God Who called you that will answer your challengers. If you are not called and you do not hide under the calling of the person that is called, you will not be able to withstand the challenges that go along with Christian Drama Communications. If you are not able to withstand it, there would be a backfire in drama presentations. In other words, the negative roles that are played by people, including the use of negative words can take their tolls on the performers. It can even result into deaths. I am sure no one would like to get involved in what can cause his death. My experience while producing serial movies in 1999 proves the reality of backfire.

In 1 Corinthians 1: 26-29, the Bible says, ***"For ye see your calling, brethren, how that not many wise men after the flesh, not many mighty, not many noble, are called: But God hath chosen the foolish things of the world to confound the wise; and God hath chosen the weak things of the world to confound the things which are mighty; And base things of the world, and things which are despised, hath God chosen, yea, and things which are not, to bring to nought things that are: That no flesh should glory in his presence."***

We can see a number of things in the above passage. God always bypass the wise and pick those who are considered foolish by the world. He picks the weak to perform mighty things like the case of David who was used by God to bring down Goliath that threatened Israel even though there are great soldiers. He chose those who are despised to show forth His glory like the case of Jabez in 1 Chronicle 4:9-10 and build someone who is regarded as nobody into a great person like Jehoshaphat in 1 King chapter 22. Why does God use this method? The reason is through that no flesh would glory in His presence. If a person is called or chosen by God for a mission, the Lord will so use him that it would be obvious that the work is the Lord's doing. This is what the passage is all about.

VARIOUS SKILLS, CALLINGS AND TALENTS IN CHRISTIAN DRAMA COMMUNICATIONS

1. *SCRIPT WRITING*: This is one of if not the most crucial aspect of Christian Drama Communications. Christian Drama Communications without a drama script is like a paper presentation with paper to present or house without a planned structure or a mission without vision. A few of people may work in the secular drama productions without scripts but it hardly works in true Christian Drama Communications unless there is constant rehearsal of the play with every interpreter of roles knowing what to do or say at each sequence.

It is true that Holy Spirit may be in control of the interpreter of roles as in the case of a preacher but the human factors or emotions can make the entire production a complete failure if there is no script that would guide the actors and actresses.

Unlike a preacher who may not need to rehearsal what he would say to the audience since he is already familiar with the Bible that serves as guidance, Christian Drama Communications essentially require scripts as plans or guides in the ministrations. The person who writes drama scripts is called a script writer or playwright or screenwriter, depending if the play is for book or stage drama or film productions.

Christian script writing is a calling. It involves a lot of skills, inspiration of the Holy Spirit and deep insight into the word of God. When a Christian who is called into scripting writes a story which is well translated into a movie, it always touches lives. When the first drama script which I was inspired to write was translated into a movie titled: "The black worshippers" in 1997, it made quite an impact even in the secular world. The movie was used to fight cultism in schools and other places. It never won any award but when it was exhibited in some schools in Lagos; Ogun and Oyo states in Nigeria then. Most of the students always responded to the gospel message in the movie by giving their lives to Jesus. I remember how thousands of students in Mayflower Secondary School in Ikenne-Remo gathered round me for counseling after the film show in 1998. It was awesome. The film proves it to me that souls can be led to Christ through drama. Of course, it can also be used to destroy lives if the message in the story id destructive.

Scripts for Christian Drama Communications must be inspired by the Holy Spirit before the movies can make godly impact in the lives of the viewers.

Everybody have got at least one good story to tell but not everybody knows how to tell it. Many people know how to relate a good story for film but most of them do not have the skills to write it. As pointed earlier on, there are lots of ingredients involved in a Christian or evangelical drama scripts or screenplays which need to be thoroughly studied.

2. _DIRECTING_: This is the work of a director of either production, casting or photography. Although there are various types of directors, especially in a movie but often times only one director directs the entire production of a movie or play. In some cases, the functions of director of photography (shooting) differ from casting director or dialogue director.

Just like script writing, directing a movie or drama demands professionalism otherwise the entire production will end up in a mess. The director is the one that co-ordinate the casts in the interpretation of various roles as in the screenplay or drama script. He sees to it that the set, the casts, locations and other things are in order. He studies the scripts, audition casts for all the roles and think of the best way to translate the story into motion picture, making adjustments if there is need.

Obviously, by the nature of his functions, a director must be good in acting too and must possess the ability to lead and direct casts and production crew on what to do. Needless to point out, an amateur director can turn a good script into a bad production and a professional director can turn a faulty script into a good production.

3. PRODUCTION: A producer oversees the entire process o production of a drama or movies though he may not be skillful either in directing or acting or script writing. A good producer knows how to get a good script and a good director who at times recommend good artists for the production. As long as you have enough money to spend on productions, you can be a producer. I know of someone who became a producer and an actor that featured in his own production even though he is not so good in acting. Because he has the money to invest in it, he made a movie. I have to reserve my comment when I saw the movie so as not to discourage him. When he told me how much he invested in the production, I could not resist telling him that I can produce five movies with that amount and each of them would be better than what he has produced. Good movie productions are so expensive to make that Christians cannot afford to waste money to make one if they are not so skillful. If any Christian has money to invest in the movie production, he or she can become an executive producer and hire a professional producer to handle the entire productions. An executive producer is the owner of the production.

4. ACTING: Some people have argued whether acting is a calling or not or whether everybody is gifted in acting or not. The answer to that is simple enough. To answer the question, we need to study the opening story of the missionary team that acted the story of Jesus Christ. Unknown to many people, everybody in this world is an actor or actress. Let me share with you what happened in the Church where I am the pastor. I observed that many people do not always dance while praising God. When it was time for me to preach, I asked the congregation if God has done anything worth celebrating since they were born. They all agreed that God has done so many great things in their lives since they were born. I told them of the need to celebrate what God has done for them so far instead of thinking of what He is yet to do. I further told them that they should sing and dance to God if they want Him to perform more miracles in their lives. Everybody danced so well that I marveled. After dancing, I told them to shout Hallelujah. The shouts were deafening. This is acting! I simply direct the people to act even though they did not feel like. Here we can see that anybody can act if he or she sees reason to act. The missionary team saw reasons to act and they acted the story of Jesus. At the very least, the actor can act himself.

Acting is not actually a difficult thing. It becomes difficult for some people, however, if they are told to act someone else who has the personality that may be different from theirs. If you can act any personality, however difficult, and can get close to it in resemblance, then you're a good actor or actress.

Another thing that can make acting difficult is merging actions and dialogues together while interpreting a role along side with someone else. In that wise, it would be hard to be natural unless you are good in acting. Most professional scripts writers provide guides in the form of narratives on how the actor or actress is expected to react before, during or after a particular dialogue. Where some scripts do not indicate this, the role interpreters would have to use their initiatives. Some drama productions do not have scripts at all. Although that does not mean that a good drama cannot be staged if there are good actors and actresses on ground but in movie, which is more complicated to produce, the process of production would go wrong if there is no script to guide the actors or actresses, director, the costumier, the location manger and other production crew.

During the auditioning, the director or producer often looks for the best material for a particular role. Sometimes they find it hard to pick which material to use for each role. So they focus their attention on the skill, stamina, ability to render a long dialogue without mistakes and the composure of the candidate for the role. If he or she can get the attention of the director in these areas, he or she may win a thick role for him or herself.

THE BASIC QUALITIES OF A TRUE DRAMA MINISTER.

It is not enough to be talented or called as a drama minister for all these do not make a person a true drama minister. We are going to consider the basic qualities of a true drama minister.

i. TRUE DRAMA MINISTERS ARE SAVED: Since the minister through Christian Drama Communication is telling people about Jesus and the kingdom of God, he must be born-again. Jesus said to Nicodemus and everybody in the world in John 3:3 that unless you are born-again, you cannot see the kingdom of God. Invariably, before anyone can be in the position to point others to the Kingdom of God, he too must know and be ready to go to the place. If a drama minister is unregenerate (not born-again), he can easily mislead others with his or her performances or his conduct or lifestyle. The Bible says in 1 Peter 1:23, *"Being born again, not of corruptible seed, but of incorruptible, by the word of God, which liveth and abideth forever."* We can see that drama minster that is not born-again is of corruptible seed and corruptible seed will corrupt other seeds like the people that are watching him or her. A lot of people wrongly assume that a person is qualified to be a minister in any capacity once he or she can act or can speak very well. It is also erroneous belief to assume that drama and many other ministers are the same. The sad thing is that most ministers we see around are not regenerated even though they preach, pray, act or even prophecy. The big question now is: how do you know them? To answer the question, let us consider what Jesus said in Matthew 7:15-17, *"Beware of false prophets, which come to you in sheep's clothing, but inwardly they are ravening wolves. Ye shall know them by their fruits. Do men gather grapes of thorns, or figs of thistles? Even so every good tree bringeth forth good fruit; but a corrupt tree bringeth forth evil fruit."* Thus through the fruits they bear and not talents, you can know true Christians.

ii. TRUE DRAMA MINISTERS KEEP THE WORD OF GOD: Jesus said to all His disciples in John 14:15, *"If ye love me, keep my commandments."* We can see that Christians, including drama ministers must study and keep the word of God. In Psalm 119:15-17, the Bible says, *"I will meditate in thy precepts, and have respect unto thy ways. I will delight myself in thy statutes: I will not forget thy word. Deal bountifully with thy servant, that I may live, and keep thy word."* The word of God is all a believer needs before he can overcome all battles, make impact in his ministry and become successful and prosperous in everything about his or her life.

iii. <u>TRUE DRAMA MINISTERS ARE FILLED WITH THE SPIRIT OF GOD</u>: Again, Jesus said in the same passage in verse 16, *"And I will pray the Father, and he shall give you another Comforter, that he may abide with you forever…"* Here we can see that every minister must be filled with Spirit of God that would perform some functions within and through him or her. In Acts Act 1:8, the Bible says, *"But ye shall receive power, after that the Holy Ghost is come upon you: and ye shall be witnesses unto me both in Jerusalem, and in all Judaea, and in Samaria, and unto the uttermost part of the earth."* Here we can see the functions of the Holy Spirit in the life of a minister which include power to (1) live a holy life (2) live a victorious life and (3) share the word of God, performing signs and wonders; according to Mark 16:17-18, where Jesus said, **"And these signs shall follow them that believe; In my name shall they cast out devils; they shall speak with new tongues; They shall take up serpents; and if they drink any deadly thing, it shall not hurt them; they shall lay hands on the sick, and they shall recover."**

iv. <u>**TRUE DRAMA MINISTERS PREACH THE TRUTH**</u>: Again, Jesus continues in John 14:17, **"Even the Spirit of truth; whom the world cannot receive, because it seeth him not, neither knoweth him: but ye know him; for he dwelleth with you, and shall be in you."** A true drama minister must aim to preach the truth that is revealed in the word of God by the Holy Spirit. He or she must not take part in any drama that preaches heresy or anything that is not in line with the word of God. Anyone who does that is communicating the word of God but preaching against it. Since all Christians are saved and called to serve through one way or the other, preaching and living by the word of God are ways to reach out to others. Being truthful all the time are parts of the proofs that a Christian knows the truth and he or she is filled with Holy Spirit.

v. <u>**TRUE DRAMA MINISTERS USES THEIR TALENTS TO FULFIL GOD'S PURPOSE ON EARTH:**</u> The parable of Jesus Christ teaches a great deal about talents in Matthew 25:14-28. The passage reads, **"For the kingdom of heaven is as a man travelling into a far country, who called his own servants, and delivered unto them his goods. And unto one he gave five talents, to another two, and to another one; to every man according to his several ability; and** straightway took his journey. Then he that had received the five talents went and traded with the same, and made them other five talents. And likewise he that had received two, he also gained other two. But he that had received one went and digged in the earth, and hid his lord's money. After a long time the lord of those servants cometh, and reckoneth with them. And so he that had received five talents came and brought other five talents, saying, Lord, thou deliveredst unto me five talents: behold, I have gained beside them five talents more. His lord said unto him, Well done, thou good and faithful servant: thou hast been faithful over a few things, I will make thee ruler over many things: enter thou into the joy of thy lord. He also that had received two talents came and said, Lord, thou deliveredst unto me two talents: behold, I have gained two other talents beside them. His lord said unto him, Well done, good and faithful servant; thou hast been faithful over a few things, I will make thee ruler over many things: enter thou into the joy of thy lord. Then he which had received the one talent came and said, Lord, I knew thee that thou art an hard man, reaping where thou hast not sown, and gathering where thou hast not strawed: And I was afraid, and went and hid thy talent in the earth: lo, there thou hast that is thine. His lord answered and said unto him, Thou wicked and slothful servant, thou knewest that I reap where I sowed not, and gather where I have not strawed: Thou oughtest therefore to have put my money to the exchangers, and then at my coming I should have received mine own with usury. Take therefore the talent from him, and give it unto him which hath ten talents."** This passage is a proof that everybody, especially Christians is endowed with at least a talent or a gift or an ability to do something that would draw souls to Christ, giving God the glory, encouraging people with their walks with Him and leading them to heaven. The justifications or the returns for the allocations of talents that are given to each person are in terms of souls, not in terms of money. Money as a matter of fact is man invention. But a lot of gifted drama, music and other ministers use their gifts for financial benefits, fame or self glory. Many put financial or other gains ahead of other considerations for souls in their ministries. Whereas true ministers of God are not money making but soul making vessels, going by the scriptural examples.

God gives Christians talents for the purpose of expansion of His kingdom, not for financial gains. It is when they use their talents for this purpose that God blesses them financially, meeting their physical and spiritual needs, giving them good health, good homes and or other things.

It must be emphasized that everybody is talented in one thing or the other. Some may be gifted in singing while some in acting or teaching or preaching or helping others through one way or the other. Those who are not as gifted as others should not envy or compete with anyone. Instead, they should make best use of what they have. After all, God is not going to ask anyone what He has not given him or her. Christians who diligently use their talents to serve God are always blessed one way or the other.

When Christians with few talents continue to tell God what He already knows about their gifts, they are actually complaining to Him just like the servant with one talent in the parable. If, however, they use the limited talents to press towards the great commission which is evangelism as recorded in Mark 16:15, God will increase their talents, going by the parable. Paul wrote to the Philippians in chapter 3 verse 13-14, ***"Brethren, I count not myself to have apprehended: but this one thing I do, forgetting those things which are behind, and reaching forth unto those things which are before, I press toward the mark for the prize of the high calling of God in Christ Jesus."*** From the above passage, Paul recognized the fact that he has to direct all his gifts towards one goal which is the call to reach out to people. That alone made him one of if not the greatest Apostles in the history of man.

Many people may miss heaven, not because they are sinners but because they bury their talents, according to the parable. Charles Spurgeon said that if you are diligent in distributing tracts, you're likely going to be given another high calling in preaching to others in a bigger way.

If you do nothing with what you have been given, the grace and the opportunities to make exploit for the Lord would be taken away from you. They would be given to someone who already has more than enough talents. That is what Jesus means when He said in Matthew 25: 29, ***"For unto every one that hath shall be given, and he shall have abundance: but from him that hath not shall be taken away even that which he hath."***

Multi-talented Christians, however, must not feel better than others who has less talents because for one, they are prone to danger of pride which can destroy them. Secondly, they are saddled with more responsibilities that are in proportions with their gifts just like the servants with five talents in the parable. In other words, they are expected to produce more, going by the lesson in the story. Jesus said in Luke 12:48 *"...For unto whomsoever much is given, of him shall be much required: and to whom men have committed much, of him they will ask the more."* In other words Christians must justify the investments God had made inside them through their productivity because, as a matter of fact, God do allow any waste of His investments.

This aspect leads us to a crucial topic which is the question of talents in Christian Drama Communications.

CHRISTIAN DRAMA COMMUNICATION TALENTS

As earlier pointed out, everybody in this world is an actor or actress. Sometimes we act or demonstrate what we say or teach through our gestures or expressions on our faces which all form part of acting. We all act either in real life or in both fake and real life. The fake life is the drama you watch on stage or in movies. A very good example of drama in real Christian life which had earlier been referred to is found in the book of Act of Apostles 21:10-13. Let us pick the one-man drama that later became a reality. That passage reads, **"And as we tarried there many days, there came down from Judaea a certain prophet, named Agabus. And when he was come unto us, he took Paul's girdle, and bound his own hands and feet, and said, Thus saith the Holy Ghost, So shall the Jews at Jerusalem bind the man that owneth this girdle, and shall deliver him into the hands of the Gentiles. And when we heard these things, both we, and they of that place, besought him not to go up to Jerusalem. Then Paul answered, What mean ye to weep and to break mine heart? for I am ready not to be bound only, but also to die at Jerusalem for the name of the Lord Jesus."**

We can see a prophet named Agabus taking Paul's belt and acted or demonstrated how Paul would be treated at Jerusalem. Everybody got the message but Paul refused to be persuaded not to go. The prophecy came to pass; according the rest of the chapter of the passage. Charles Spurgeon said that the Act of Apostles was written because the Apostles acted. Hence, we have the basis to say everybody in this world is an actor or actress. Now the question is: what do we do in playing our roles in the real or fake life drama?

THE DRAMA TALENT: To appreciate or find an answer to the question above, we must understand what talent in drama is about. Apart from the scripting, directing and other aspects of drama that require skills, the drama talent is actually in the form of acting. Again, as pointed out earlier, everybody can at least act his or her personality if he or she is not conscious that people are watching. In reality show for instance, people act themselves very well more than in fake life show as in movies.

What is actually required as a talent, especially in Christian Drama Communications is the ability to act oneself or someone else whether people are watching or not. When people watch you, you will feel they are judging your performance. Because nobody likes to be judged, especially in a negative way, they do everything to avoid being judged.

The feelings of being judged is what makes people shy from others. In a situation like that, it is hard if not impossible for a person to act even himself. When you find it hard to act yourself because you are conscious people are watching you, you may assume that you are not talented in acting although that does not really mean you are not. If, however, you are able to overcome your shyness or what is known as stage fright, which is usually caused by the consciousness that people are watching or judging you, you will see that you can act. Another thing is that if you are good at hiding your true colour, then you are a good actor or actress. Also if you can really be yourself without caring about what people think, you are also good in acting. If you can also pretend to be what you are not, you are also a good actor or actress. Note that being a good or bad actor does not mean a person is playing a good or bad role in real or fake life. Rather the terms describe the quality way the person is playing the roles in real or fake life. There are lots of good actors and actresses that are playing high quality roles in secular movies, most of which are spreading bad and even destructive messages around the world. This is one of the main reasons Christians must counter these messages by going into Christian Drama Communications. If they leave secular world to continue to send destructive messages around the world, they would have more and more people turning into enemies of God who pose serious threats to human lives. We can attribute the violent movies as the major influence that turns lots of people, especially youths into violent people.

DEVELOPING DRAMA TALENTS: Now that you know you can act, how do you develop the talent in you? We will consider a few steps.
1. The first step to be taken if you are serious about by getting involved in Christian Drama Communications is to begin from

where you are either in the Church or other places. In the course of that, you acquire experience or knowledge or information about the ministry. This will usher you into further steps even when the going gets tough. There are so many drama ministries that started very well. They seem to be making impact until they cannot withstand the test of time. Do not take any step at all until you are sure you want to go into it with pure, sincere heart and the burden to reach out to souls.

2. After you got the burden or vision or revelation, you must develop interest in Christian Drama Communications. It is your keen interest that would earn you the opportunities you need to move forward. If you lack interest in anything, needless to say, you cannot move beyond the level of indifference. This invariably leads to nowhere but failure. The development of the interest must be tailored towards the vision or burden. As pointed earlier, there are different areas in Christian Drama Communications such as scripting, directing, story idea etc. A lot of people think they are good in scripting but, in reality, they are more of script enthusiasts than script writers. Note again: The hallmark of a good Christian script writer is the ability to preach the balance word of God through drama scripting. You may be called into Christian drama but not into script writing. In that case, you act as the script or director directs you to act.

3. The next step is to be a student or an apprentice or a follower of a reputable drama minister. A lot of people assume that once they are gifted in drama, they can gather other people and then begin the Christian Drama Communications. This is a major risk. It is like a case of an untrained soldier who feels he is gifted in using weapons. Thus he can invite other people to team up with him and launch out an attack against experienced enemies. The enemies who have different weapons are invisible. So they see the inexperienced soldiers as bunch of school children that walk around wild animals. They are simply meat for their enemies. I know a lot of people who went into the ministries they are not trained for, losing their callings; salvation or even their lives. These people probably do not understand that all true ministries are platforms to engage the enemies in the battle. They have to be trained through one way or the other before they are really fit for battles. The Bible says in Ephesians 6:12, **"For we wrestle not against flesh and blood, but against principalities, against powers, against the rulers of the darkness of this world,**

against spiritual wickedness in high places." Going by this passage, there are four categories of these enemies that are not flesh and blood. They are 1. Principalities 2. Powers 3. Rulers of Darkness 4. Spiritual Wickedness. The inexperienced soldiers can easily be brought down by the lowest rank of enemies (Principalities) which mainly use the flesh as weapons.

Christian Drama Communication ministries are not fun or entertainment industries at all. They are means or platforms to preach the living word of God. When drama ministers understand this, they will know that they need the whole (not part of) the armor of God as in verses 14 to 20. Since Christian Drama Communications, just like other ministries, are platforms to attack the enemies by exposing them or preaching the word of God, there is hierarchy of authority which flows from Jesus to the Christian soldiers through the leaders. The centurion proved that he understood the principle of soldiering when he said to Jesus in Matthew 8:9, *"For I am a man under authority, having soldiers under me: and I say to this man, Go, and he goeth; and to another, Come, and he cometh; and to my servant, Do this, and he doeth it."*

In verse 10, the Bible says, *"When Jesus heard it, he marvelled, and said to them that followed, Verily I say unto you, I have not found so great faith, no, not in Israel.."* This passage indicates that Jesus acknowledged the fact that physical soldering is very much the same as the spiritual ones.

Occupying the position of spiritual authority which a person is not prepared or trained for is like courting with spiritual troubles and deaths, which can be brought down into the physical. If man will be smart enough to place a well trained person to lead an army in the physical battle, how would anyone expect God to place untrained person to lead Christian soldiers in spiritual battles that will determine so many eternal lives? It is instructive, therefore, to note that just because a person is gifted, talented or even spiritually strong does not qualify him to be the leader. Even if a person has leadership potentials, he still has to go through training. The bottom line is: to be a good leader; you must also be a good follower. To be a good commander of soldiers, you must be a cadet, to be a good teacher, you must be a good student and to be a good master, you must be a good servant.

When you know you are supposed to be in the classroom as a student who is undergoing some training, you will not attempt to be a leader by forming a team that would launch battles against the enemies who know so much about you, including your weak areas. In fact, attempting to be a leader when you are supposed to a follower is like climbing a ladder from the top. Anyone who attempts that would find himself on the ground with wounds.

Having established the above facts, you need to find a reputable minister whose ministry can accommodate your vision or a revelation or burden and stay under his calling. Even if he does not have a drama ministry, you can share the vision with him. A lot of ministers do not know that they can be more effective in their ministries either in the Church or outside if they give room for Christian Drama Communications. Of course, if the minister buys into the vision, you must be under his authority until God says and confirms that you can be on your own. Even if you are on your own, you still need someone to lead or coach or mentor you. Like someone said, you become too dangerous to yourself and other people if you are left on your own.

4. The next step is constant rehearsals. Rehearsals cannot be compromised with. It is a law that must not be violated in anyway. Since Christian Drama Communications are more of practical than theoretical studies, you learn to perform very well by rehearsing or acting constantly. Constant practice is the hallmark of perfection in almost all professions. As explained earlier, everybody can act but people become experts in Christian Drama Communications when they rehearse constantly. Some of the things you learn consciously or unconsciously when you are involved in constant drama rehearsal includes (i) ability to act the personality that is different from yours (ii) ability to overcome stage fright and (iii) ability to dominate the opinions of audience; especially if you are interpreting the role people hate or do not agree with.

I took the lead role in one of my movies titled The Black Worshippers in 1997. I interpreted the role of a cultist who was sent to get the heads of two Christian sisters. My wife took the movie to her friend to watch it with her and her neighbours when it was newly released. Many people watched it with excitements. As I went to perform the assignment given to me by the cult leaders, putting so much effort into the drama so as to make it look real, the audience angrily called me all sorts of names you can imagine. My wife's friend looked at her, expecting her to react. She only smiled, making her to understand that someone has to act the bad guy so that the people can get the message in the movie. At the end of the movie, most of them gave their lives to Christ. The same thing happened when the movie was used to expose deadly effect of cultism in many secondary schools and campuses in Nigeria.

It is almost impossible to overcome all the huddles in reaching professionalism without constant rehearsals. More often than not the performance of an amateur can easily be distinguished from that of a professional by the audience that are used to watching good drama. The action, facial expressions and other things while interpreting a role will indicate if the actor or actress has been acting for long or not. It is easy for a professional director to know how good person is during auditioning. For instance, if you are acting on a stage or in the Church and you often back the audience, a professional will know that both the drama director and the actor are amateurs.

5. Constant prayer meetings and fellowships are crucial in Christian Drama Communications. In 1 Thessalonians 5:17, the Bible says, ***"pray without ceasing."*** In other words, every Christian, including various ministers must constantly pray. Paul said in Philippians, ***"I thank my God upon every remembrance of you, Always in every prayer of mine for you all making request with joy, For your fellowship in the gospel from the first day until now; Being confident of this very thing, that he which hath begun a good work in you will perform it until the day of Jesus Christ:"***

From the above passage, we understand the need for prayers and fellowship so that the good works may continue. Through constant prayers and fellowship with one another who are in the same drama ministries, battles are fought and won together through prayers even before the team launch out. One of the reasons fellowship is required is for the purpose of sharing the word of God that would make everybody grow in the spirit. The Spirit of unity is always present when true believers gathered together in the name of the Lord. The Spirit of unity is very required in every ministry, including drama if the ministers want to do the work of the Lord or to make any meaningful progress. If you take a piece of broom, you can easily break it but try to break a bunch of broom and see the result. As no one can break a bunch of broom, no enemy can break any member of the united soldiers of Jesus.

CONCLUSION: Having gone through this course, Christian Drama Communications, you need to be more involved in constant rehearsals and fellowships. In other words, the next step is to go into the practical aspect since Christian Drama Communication is more of a practical than theoretical work.

Assessment Questions

1. Use passages in the Bible to establish the basis of Christian Drama Communications.
2. Explain the characteristics of true Christian Drama Communications.
3. Explain each of the motives and callings of a true Drama Minister.
4. Explain the various skills, callings and talents in Christian Drama Communications.
5. Explain each of the basic qualities of a true Drama Minister.
6. Explain Drama Talents and steps to be taken before they can be developed.

CHRISTIAN MUSICAL COMMUNICATIONS

BOOK THREE

INTRODUCTION

The ministry of music or song is the only ministry that will last till eternity. So everybody must be involved in it, at least for the purposes which would later be explained. In the book of Revelation 14:1-4, the Bible says, **"And I looked, and, lo, a Lamb stood on the mount Sion, and with him an hundred forty and four thousand, having his Father's name written in their foreheads. And I heard a voice from heaven, as the voice of many waters, and as the voice of a great thunder: and I heard the voice of harpers harping with their harps: And they sung as it were a new song before the throne, and before the four beasts, and the elders: and no man could learn that song but the hundred and forty and four thousand, which were redeemed from the earth. These are they which were not defiled with women; for they are virgins. These are they which follow the Lamb whithersoever he goeth. These were redeemed from among men, being the firstfruits unto God and to the Lamb."**

Here the Bible talks about redeemed people, singing in the voices of many waters like the voice of loud thunder in heaven. There were also instrumentalists with them. They sang song as if it were new before the throne. So many passages in the Bible establishes song ministry as both universal and eternal ministry.

Christian Musical Communication is not only an emotional but also a spiritual means to accomplish so many things in life and in eternity. We, therefore, want to study this vital course in line with the scriptures before going into the practical.

As a first step into this course, it is instructive to note that everybody in this world can sing and every believer must be involved in the Christian Musical Communications. Consciously or unconsciously, when we sing praises to God, we are actually involved in Christian Musical Communications. We shall divide the studies into five parts which are (i) song writing (ii) melody writing (iii) instrumentation (iv) vocalization and (v) directing.

Note that all these do not necessary needs to be in place before a song can be composed but these aspects are the basic ones that are common.

Before we study all these aspects, let us consider six major things we do with Christian Musical Communications.

MINISTRY TO THE LORD: In John 4:23, **"But the hour cometh,**

and now is, when the true worshippers shall worship the Father in spirit and in truth: for the Father seeketh such to worship him." Songs are used to worship and praise God. When Christians praise and worship God with songs, they are actually communicating and ministering to the Lord in the Spirit. Just like in the old testaments when the people of Israel used bulls and other animals to sacrifice or to minister to the Lord, Christians use songs to offer sacrifices to the Lord. A song that explains this very well goes like this.

> *We bring the sacrifice of praise*
> *Into the house of the Lord...*
> *As we offer unto the thee...*

David is good at ministering to the Lord with songs. In Psalm 92:1-3, David wrote, *"It is a good thing to give thanks unto the LORD, and to sing praises unto thy name, O most High: To shew forth thy lovingkindness in the morning, and thy faithfulness every night, Upon an instrument of ten strings, and upon the psaltery; upon the harp with a solemn sound."*

The simple fact that songs are major sources of giving praises and ministering to the Lord makes Christian Musical Communications vital for everybody, both young and old, male and female to be involved in.

When Christians communicate or minister to God with songs, He always responds and even reveals His mind to them as He did in Acts 13:2 which says, *"As they ministered to the Lord, and fasted, the Holy Ghost said, Separate me Barnabas and Saul for the work whereunto I have called them."* Ministering to the Lord does not necessarily means you are praying or asking God to do something for you. It is actually telling God who He is and what He has done. In verse 3 of that passage, the disciples later prayed and laid hands on Saul and Barnabas before they send them away on the assignment. Another example of the songs that are used to minister unto the Lord, which is different from that of the prayers song is found in Revelation 4:10-11 which says, *"The four and twenty elders fall down before him that sat on the throne, and worship him that liveth for ever and ever, and cast their crowns before the throne, saying:*

> *Thou art worthy, O Lord,*
> *to receive glory and honour and power:*
> *for thou hast created all things,*
> *and for thy pleasure they are and were created*

The above passage are composed into a song that is used to worship God in many Churches till today.

Another song that is composed from the old testament of the Bible is found in 1Samuel 2:2, which says:

There is none holy as the LORD:
for there is none beside thee:
neither is there any rock like our God...

QUESTION: Give examples of other songs to communicate or minister to the Lord in the Bible.

MINISTRY OF PRAYER OR INTERCESSION: The ministry of song is also used and needed in the ministry of prayer. In 1 Corinthians 14:15, Paul said, **"What is it then? I will pray with the spirit, and I will pray with the understanding also: I will sing with the spirit, and I will sing with the understanding also."**

Before Christians talk to God in prayers, it is necessary for them to first communicate to Him through songs of praises, adoration and appreciation. Such songs create a conducive atmosphere for Holy Spirit to operates. In fact, I have personally experienced God performing miracles even before asking for them in prayers when we simply sang songs like these:

He's a miracle working God
He's the Alpha and Omega...

The wall of Jericho fell down flat
When children of God are praising the Lord...

Keep me, Jesus
As the apple of your eyes
Hide under the shadow of your wings...

There are so many songs like that which are meant to pray. When you use songs to pray, prayer becomes easy - so easy that you can be praying unconsciously while you think you are singing. Using song to pray also makes prayer exciting and lively with spiritual exercise.

QUESTION: Give example of songs for prayer.

PREACHING AND EVANGELICAL MINISTRY: Christian Musical Communications can also be used in preaching the gospel and reaching out to lost souls. In Mark 16:15, Jesus said to all those who believe in Him, *"Go ye into all the world, and preach the gospel to every creature."* There are so many songs can serve this purpose. Such songs include:

Come into my hearth
Lord Jesus
Come in today
Come in to stay…
Amazing grace
Who sweet the wound
That saves a wretch like me
I was once lost but now I'm found
I was blind but now I see…

What actually distinguishes one song from the other is mainly the lyrics or the wordings of the song or music. So many evangelists and preachers have used songs to pass messages around. One unique thing about using Christian Musical Communications to pass messages to the audience is that it makes people remember and even memorize it without the preacher being around. Once the people master the song, they go about singing and teaching others who also teaches others. Christian Musical Communication is one of the most effective ways people are taught the word of God. It is used to spread the message of the Lord and also used as a way people are taught how to praise and worship God.

Christian Musical Communications must be used to preach the good news otherwise the devil will use it to mislead people as music is used in the secular world. While through ungodly music brood of vipers are bred with so many people are being initiated into cults, Christian Musical Communications souls can be lead to Christ and trained to be soldiers.

MINISTRY OF WORD OF ENCOURAGEMENT AND HOPE: We live in the world that is characterized with evils, pains, sorrow, discouragement, compromise and failures. Christians, especially new converts are as vulnerable to all these things. Unless they are encouraged one way or the other, they may grow weak or even die spiritually. The man who wrote the song: "It is well with my soul" lost all his children in a ship wreck with only his wife surviving. A lot of song writers wrote their master pieces through the inspiration of Holy Spirit after they have gone through one trauma or catastrophe or the other. The Bible tells us in James 5:13, *"Is any among you afflicted? let him pray. Is any merry? let him sing psalms."* In Ephesians 5:19-20, we read like this: *"Speaking to yourselves in psalms and hymns and spiritual songs, singing and making melody in your heart to the Lord; Giving thanks always for all things unto God and the Father in the name of our Lord Jesus Christ."*

We can see it from the above passages that Christian Musical Communications can powerful and vital tools to encourage anyone going through hard times. It is little wonder David who used songs to encourage himself was able to survive the chains of calamities that fell on him right from the time he killed Goliath up to the time he was on his sick bed when he sons were fighting over his throne.

A researcher discovered that Christians are the happiest people on earth. Another one discovered that they live longer than non-Christians. The secret lies in the fact that Christians has the word of God that is composed as songs or hymns. When they sing or read them, they are encouraged.

Examples of songs of encouragement:

Dry bones shall rise again...
Lord, Jehovah is able
To do all things
He is more than able...

He has promised
He will never fail
I will hold on Him...

I have a very big God
He is always by side
A very God by my side everyday

I have a God who never fail
Who never fail forever more
Amen, Jesus never fail...

QUESTION: Give examples of songs of encouragement.

MINISTRY OF DELIVERANCE: For you to appreciate the ministry of deliverance, you need to study the course: Deliverance Methodology. In the Lord's Prayer in Matthew 6:9-14, we are taught to pray for deliverance from evil. This prayer was made into a song. The ministry of deliverance just like in most if not all other ministries require songs of deliverance. Let us take our reference in 1 Samuel 16:14-23. In that passage, you will read how king Saul was troubled by distressing spirit and how David used songs and instrument to relieve him of the spirit. Since everybody - both Christians and non-Christians need deliverance from one thing or the other, we often times need to use songs to get deliverance. If we do not constantly need deliverance, Jesus would not have taught the disciples in the Lord's Prayer, which has this clause *"to deliver us from evil."* Apart from deliverance from evils that are rampant in this world, we need deliverance from sins or temptations to sin. We need deliverance from flesh and affairs of this world. We need deliverance from battles or challenges of life like poverty, sickness, sorrow, pains and other things like that. Example of songs of deliverance:

My Lord who delivered Daniel…
Why not deliver me?

Come down, oh, Lord
And manifest your power…

QUESTION: Give examples of songs of deliverance.

SONGS ARE USED TO BRING JOY TO TH SINGERS AND AUDIENCE: The Bible says in Nehemiah 8:10 that the joy of the Lord is the strength of all believers. There are songs that are composed to bring joy into hearts of the people. The world is full of sorrow and emotional pains that dampen the spirit of man but Christian Musical Communications can be used to bring joy into the people. Since joy of the Lord is the strength of believers, it follows therefore that they must always sing joyful songs if they want to be joyful always. Without the joy of the Lord, a Christian may grow weak spiritually and emotionally. Weakness in any of any these areas can brings about depression and even sickness. This can make him vulnerable to the arrows of the devil, making him feel that life is not worth living.

Songs of joy play great roles in the life of Christians.

Examples of songs of joy are:

Melody in my heart today, today
Rise up melody in my heart...

The joy of the Lord
Is my strength...

I will sing unto the Lord
A joyful and praise His name
For the Lord is good...

QUESTIONS: Give examples of songs that bring joy to people.

SONGS ARE USED TO FIGHT SPIRITUAL BATTLES: In 2 Corinthians 10:3-5, the Bible says. *"For though we walk in the flesh, we do not war after the flesh: (For the weapons of our warfare are not carnal, but mighty through God to the pulling down of strong holds;) Casting down imaginations, and every high thing that exalteth itself against the knowledge of God, and bringing into captivity every thought to the obedience of Christ."* Whether we know it or not, everybody faces battles everyday. Although these battles each person faces may differ from one another, Christian Musical Communications can be used to fight battles. As I have it in one of my books titled: "The Battle Of the Conquerors," everybody fights in these three battle fields: The body(Physical), the mind (Emotional) and the spirit (Spiritual). The one in the body may be physical like sickness, poverty, lust of the flesh and lust of the eyes. The battles in the mind may include evil thoughts, fear in various forms, pride and other things that exist in the mind. The battles in the spirit are essentially spiritual problems like that of demonic depressions, oppressions and possessions of people. Songs can be used to fight these battles, especially if Christians constantly sing this type of songs. As they sing the song, they fight the battles with ease, praying without knowing it.

Examples of such songs is:

By the anointing
Jesus brings the yoke
By the Holy Ghost and power
Just as the prophets foretold
This is the day of the later
God is moving with His power again
By the anointing
Jesus brings the joke
It's not by power
It's not by might

We are able to go up
And take the country
To possess the land of Judah
To the sea
Though the giants
May be on our way to hinder
God will surely give us victory
So move on to the righteous side
Move to the righteous side of God...

QUESTION: Give examples of songs use to fight battles.

SONGS ARE USED TO REMIND CHRISTIANS OF HEAVEN: This is one if not the most important purpose of Christian Musical Communications on earth. Jesus said in John 14:2-3, *"in my Father's house are many mansions: if it were not so, I would have told you. I go to prepare a place for you. And if I go and prepare a place for you, I will come again, and receive you unto myself; that where I am, there ye may be also."*

It is easy to forget this important passage which all believers need to think about all the time even when going through problems. The reality of death comes to people only when they lose someone close to them. So it is usually only at the funeral that songs that remind people of heaven are sung. When people sing such songs, often times they consider the songs as customary thing to do instead of thinking deeply on the lyrics. There are lots of songs that remind people of heaven but there is one song that was composed by Jim Reeves (1923-1664) who died in a plane crash. It was as if he knew he did not have a long life when he composed and sang the song which goes like this:

This world is not my home
I'm just passing through
My treasures are laid up
Somewhere beyond the blue
The angels beckon me
From heaven's open door
And I can't feel at home
In this world anymore

Oh Lord, You know
I have no friend like You
If heaven is not my home
Then Lord what will I do?
The angels beckon me
From heaven's open door
And I can't feel at home
In this world anymore

I have a loving mother
Just over in glory land
And I don't expect to stop
Until I shake her hand
She is waiting now for me
In heaven's open door
And I can't feel at home
In this world anymore...

QUESTION: Give examples of songs that reminds people of heaven.

Songs can also be used for other things like bringing to memories heroic deeds of people in the Bible and other heroes of faiths. Christian Musical Communications as a matter of fact is a creative way of communicating to all categories of people, including children. It is so effective and influential that they can be used to lead people on the path of life or used to mislead people.

THE FIVE MAJOR AREAS OF CHRISTIAN MUSICAL COMMUNICATIONS

It is instructive to note that this course can treated with Christian Drama Communications because they have a few things in common. One of the things they have in common is that everybody is consciously or unconsciously involved in music and drama communications. Apart from this, the two ministries require scripting, directing, artistes and production crew, especially if they are to be presented in videos or movies. These creative method of communications can be said to be interwoven because they complement each other. Where there is music, there is usually some element of acting like singing, laughing or dancing or even crying which may be said to be melodramatic in a musical video. You sometimes find people acting or trying to depict the message in the song through drama. Also you will hardly find a movie without song or what they call sound track. Apart from all these, the two methods of communications can easily be used to pass messages to people. If the message comes in the form of songs, they can sing or hear and if the message is dramatized, they can watch it on stages or on videos. This is one of the reasons the dance drama an effective way of communications because it combines both music and drama to carry the people along.

The five major areas of Christian Musical Communications are not all essentially professional areas though they all require certain skills or talents before there can productions of songs that are acceptable to an average audience.

SONG WRITING: Anyone who is conversant with the scriptures can be a Christian songwriter. There are so many songs that are picked from the Bible and arranged for songs. However, at the professional level, a song writer must have a poetic insight. His talents or skills always reflect in the wordings. The wordings often times provoke thoughts of anyone who listens or reads the lyrics. Years ago, a group of secular professional vocalists; melody and songwriters called Paramount Group in US came across my song lyric on the internet. They offer to get me a professional melody writer to turn the lyrics into a song and get professional vocalist to sing it. We enter into a deal. The song was produced. It was aired in America radio stations. That was all I could achieve with the song which is to pass the message across to the people. The son is titled: It Takes Faith. It goes like this:

It takes faith to get miracles
It takes belief to get blessings
It takes tough people to get to the Promised Land
It takes joy in the Lord to overcome sorrow
It takes patience to get your needs met
It takes hope to see the Lord
It takes determination to do the will of God
It takes perseverance to possess the land
It takes doubt to lose everything
It takes unbelief to get lost...

If you study the lyrics, you will discover that so much is said within few lines. In fact, I can write a book on each of the lines, using the scriptures to support the points. For instance in first verse, the song indicates the fact that when you need a miracle, all you need is faith in God. The second verse points out that if you want God to bless you, you would need to believe in Jesus Christ because God would not bless unbelievers. And the third verse says that you would have to be spiritually tough if you want to get to heaven which is represented by the words: Promised Land in the song. The rest of the verses can easily be interpreted with the scriptures. It must be noted, however, that Christian Musical Communications require that all lyrics must be simple enough for everybody to understand since each song is designed for one or more purposes that had been studied so far.

Christians are desperately needed to be songwriters who will fight the bad influence of secular songs. To test yourself if you are a potential Christian songwriter, you can pick one of the verses of my song: "It Takes Faith" above as a topic and write your own song. If you are not all that talented in song-writing, you do not have to feel bad about yourself. I am sure there is something you can still do about in one of the other areas of the Christian Musical Communications. So let us go to the next area which you may good at.

MELODY WRITING: This is actually putting into or finding a tune for a song lyrics or wordings. Some people are good in this area while some are not. If you are gifted in getting a tune into a song, you are almost good in music generally even if you are not good at writing a song. A Christian melody writer is considered a composer in Christian Musical Communications. At the very least, he or she can get verses in the Bible and turn them into songs. It is a great gift if he or she is also good at writing the lyrics. I have the privilege to be a songwriter and poet but not good at melody writing like the professional in paramount group who wrote the melody of my song above. More often then not, I use the melody of other songs like the one in the hymn and well known songs of praises to tune my songs in the books I write for children and youths. Take for instance the song in the book: Foundation Bible Club A-Z Story book with the song titled: I will read my Bible. I used the tune of the song titled "Rock of Ages Cleft for me" to compose the song. Try using the tune to sing the song. It goes like this:

I will read my Bible
If I want to grow in Christ
I must obey what I read
If I want to live Christ
I will always preach the word
So that souls many come to Christ

Yes it is as simple as that. Anybody who can sing "Rock of Ages" would be able to sing the song above. Do NOT let anybody make you feel that Christian Musical Communications or Christian Drama Communications or anything you want to do for the Lord is a hard thing to do.

I use to tell people that everything in life is all about creativity. What seems like a mistake by you can be used by God to add value to your work. There is no way you can fail if you are filled with Holy Spirit and ready to make exploits for the Lord. You will make mistakes as you acquire relevant skills in your ministries because that is part of the training process.

ASSIGNMENT: Test your ability in melody writing by finding a Bible passage and compose it into a song.

INSTRUMENTATION: As the name connotes, it is the instrumental accomplishment of a song or music. Since musical communications is meant to be used by all Christians, including professionals, we have to leave this aspect, including the arrangements to the professional instrumentalists while we focus on other things. With the advent of technology, however, even the instrumental accomplishment is not a big issue. So do not let the so called professionals make you feel that without them, you cannot produce a good song. All you need is to go digital with your music.

There are computer software now that can perform virtually everything you want to do in music productions, including turning a male voice into female and female's into male's. The software makes it possible for one singer to produce an album all alone with the sound engineer, with or without back up.

As there are different types of music instruments and different types of music, Christian music or songs whether contemporary or classic is completely different from secular. Depending on the purpose of the song, Gospel music has different styles or types like worship songs and praises as opposed to some secular types that are out of tunes. There are so many ways you can categorize music generally but for our convenience, we can classify Gospel songs into three which can be soft, middle and fast tempo. If you are a professional musician, this classification may not be acceptable to you but remember we are talking about every Christian being involved in Christian Musical Communications either at professional or layman level.

ASSIGNMENT: Try singing a song with the instruments in a keyboard, record it and play it to someone who can objectively criticize the production.

VOCALIZATION: This is actually the voicing or singing of the song, especially by the lead voice. There are some people who go for voice training before they can sing effectively. While this is essential for some, it is not necessary for some. What is important in voicing a song is constant rehearsal of the song. Once the vocalists are able to sing the song well enough, they can go to the studio where their voices can be well treated with some computer software. The important thing in vocalization is you master the lyrics and the melody, preparing your voice as best as you can. With the power of Holy Spirit in us, we can sing like professional singers

CONCLUSION

Having gone through this course, it is believed that you are convinced that music ministry is what all Christians must be involved. If they do not get involved, the enemy of mankind will use songs to deceive and cart precious souls to hell. Since the Lord have mandated us to go into all the world to preach the gospel to every creature, each Christian is mandated to begin to communicate the word of God to everybody, including children through every means of communications, including

Christian Musical Communications.

Assessment Questions
1. Use Bible passages to establish six major things a person can use Christian Musical Communications to do.
2. Explain five major areas of Christian Musical Communications.

CHRISTIAN ORAL COMMUNICATIONS

BOOK FOUR

INTRODUCTION

There are three essential elements in the management of an organization. They are materials, manpower and money. These are the three big Ms in the management that bring about the existence and survival of any organization. Without any of these, there cannot be an organization.

However, there is one big M that is more powerful though not more important any of the others. This M is manpower. Manpower is so powerful that is can combine or manipulate other two for positive or negative result.

Manpower is the brain behind the effective workings of other Ms. For this reason, this course: Christian Human Resources concentrates solely on manpower resources. The mismanagement of human resources automatically leads to mismanagement of resources of an organization. Proper management of human resources is what will guarantee proper management of other resources like money and material resources.

DEFINITION OF CHRISTIAN HUMAN RESOURCES

There had been as many definitions of Human Resources as the number of text books available on the topic. However, for the strict purpose of this course, we shall define Christian Human Resources (CHR) as the effective use and co-ordination of the inputs of human beings who are assumed as Christians so as to get the maximum output. In other words, it is a way of making human beings in a Christian organization or ministries to put on their maximum inputs so as to get the best result. Bible says in Matthew 9:37 ***"Then saith he (Jesus) unto his disciples, The harvest truly is plenteous, but the labourers are few..."*** Since there are few labourers, Jesus cannot afford to waste or mismanage the Christian Human Resources.

When talking of Christian Human Resources (CHR), we are talking of the mental, physical, emotional and spiritual aspects of the people, especially Christians within an organization. For instance, if you can establish a business organization with N1m worth of capital, including the cost of materials, working capital and human resources. This amount can double within a year if the employees are very effective, co-operative and productive. On the after hand, this amount can evaporate within a short time without achieving a thing if the human resources are not well handled. If the workers are obsessed with their own goals instead of the collective visions of the business or organization or if they do not care about the collective vision, they can paralyze or cripple or even kill the organization. A group of people with zeal to carry out a vision will always succeed even if there are no much potentials of success in the work. If people are influenced to be focused, putting their mental, physical, emotional and spiritual aspects of their lives into proper perspectives, they will give the best of themselves. In fact, there is no room to failure in their mission unless of course if the mission itself is a failure. A case that proves is the story of Tower Of Babel in the book of Genesis 11:1-9

HUMAN DESIRES IN MANPOWER RESOURCES

Professor John Dewey, a profound philosopher says that the deepest in human nature is "desire to be important". Although, this may not be true in all cases, especially in some Christians whose ultimate desire or urge is to serve the Lord with everything they possessed. There are many case studies that establish fact. The case of elderly woman who was an usher in the Church is good to study. This old woman took it as her sole duty to pray for the Pastor and the people in the Church, asking for miracles in their lives. The Church always experienced miracles. When this elderly woman passed on, the miracles ceased. It was a terrible experience for the Pastor because no one knew that the prayer of this old woman was behind the miracles. The Pastor prayed and fasted, asking the Lord why the miracles stopped in the Church. It was then revealed to him by God and confirmed by her family member that it was the woman who had all along been praying and fasting for the miracles. Since she is with Him, there was no one that was ready to stand in the gap as the intercessor.

To some extent, we can say Dewey is right. Just like secular human resources, Christian Human Resources does not expect everybody to behave in same way. So most Christians are not like the old woman who saw it as her duty to bless others through her prayers. Again, most people including many Christians desire to be important or recognized for their good performances. This may not necessarily constitute any sin or pride. It is natural for people expect recognition of their achievements or efforts. Thus recognition of good works can serve as encouragement or incentive rather than to consider it as an ego in Christian Human Resources .

For the purpose of general studies on human attributes, let us see what Dale Carnegie enumerated as things most people, including many Christians desire in life. They are (1) Health and preservation of life. (2) Food (3) Sleep (4) Money and the things money will buy (5)

Life in the hereafter (6) Sexual gratification (7) Welfare of their children (8) A feeling of importance.

It must be admitted that the above bear some tragic truths in the attitudes of human beings. It is tragic because these are not the biblical ways. The way of the Lord is completely different as Isaiah 55:8. The passage says, *"For my thoughts are not your thoughts, neither are your ways my ways, saith the LORD."* Christians are expected to live sacrificial lives in the use of their time, possessions, money and services. But then most Christians are always concerned with what is going to be their earthly profits. Whereas the Bible says in Romans 12:1, *"I beseech you therefore, brethren, by the mercies of God, that ye present your bodies a living sacrifice, holy, acceptable unto God, which is your reasonable service."*

I shared the vision of certain work of evangelism with two fine Christian brothers. I was confused when the first question they asked me was what was going to be their gains. I was confused because I had worked for three years in a Church children ministry, which many consider to be a difficult job without earning anything. In fact, I had to contribute into the work financially myself because I could hardly find the people who are willing to make continual sacrifices of their time and money. So Dale Carnegie is right but this is not the way it ought to be for those who are true Christians.

In Christian Human Resource, this is the order: (1) The desire to serve the Lord (2) The desire to share life with family and (3) The desire to share life with other people in the community, nation and the world, depending on how much God have invested into the life of the Christian.

The desire to serve the Lord: I ask some people at a seminar where I was invited to teach some ministers. I asked them this question: If God ask you this question: *"Why Should I keep You Alive,"* how would you answer? A lady was bold enough to say, *"I would tell God to spare my life for the sake of my children."* I asked her, *"What makes you think the children cannot survive even without you?"* Nobody could answer the question. The reason most people find it hard to answer this question is that they are yet to understand the purposes of their lives. Contrary to general opinions, life is not designed to be enjoyed, especially at the expense of others. It is designed to serve God. When a person serves God with his life, he tends to enjoy it and even live long as in 2 King 201-6, which says, *"In those days was Hezekiah sick unto death. And the prophet Isaiah the son of Amoz came to him, and said unto him, Thus saith the*

LORD, Set thine house in order; for thou shalt die, and not live. Then he turned his face to the wall, and prayed unto the LORD, saying, I beseech thee, O LORD, remember now how I have walked before thee in truth and with a perfect heart, and have done that which is good in thy sight. And Hezekiah wept sore. And it came to pass, afore Isaiah was gone out into the middle court, that the word of the LORD came to him, saying, Turn again, and tell Hezekiah the captain of my people, Thus saith the LORD, the God of David thy father, I have heard thy prayer, I have seen thy tears: behold, I will heal thee: on the third day thou shalt go up unto the house of the LORD. And I will add unto thy days fifteen years; and I will deliver thee and this city out of the hand of the king of Assyria; and I will defend this city for mine own sake, and for my servant David's sake."

The above passage proves that if a person uses his life to serve God, he or she can prolong it and get God to change His mind even if He decides to terminate it.

The desire to share life with family: Since life is also designed to be shared with family like spouses, parents and children, Christians must always aspire and determine to share their lives with them even though circumstances sometimes dictate otherwise. In 1 Timothy 5:8 *"But if any provide not for his own, and especially for those of his own house, he hath denied the faith, and is worse than an infidel."*

The desire to share life with other people: Life is also designed by God to be shared with other people, especially the needy people in the community, the nation and even all over the world. There is a case of a rich man who refused to share his belongings with others let alone his life in Luke 12:16-21. The passage says, *"And he (Jesus) spake a parable unto them, saying, The ground of a certain rich man brought forth plentifully: And he thought within himself, saying, What shall I do, because I have no room where to bestow my fruits? And he said, This will I do: I will pull down my barns, and build greater; and there will I bestow all my fruits and my goods. And I will say to my soul, Soul, thou hast much goods laid up for many years; take thine ease, eat, drink, and be merry. But God said unto him, Thou fool, this night thy soul shall be required of thee: then whose shall those things be, which thou hast provided? So is he that layeth up treasure for himself, and is not rich toward God."* The story continues in Luke 16:20-24, which says, *"And there was a certain beggar named Lazarus, which was laid* *at his gate, full of sores, And desiring to be fed with the crumbs which fell from the rich man's table: moreover the dogs came and licked his sores. And it came to pass, that the beggar died, and was carried by the angels into Abraham's bosom: the rich man also died, and was buried; And in hell he lift up his eyes, being in torments, and seeth Abraham afar off, and Lazarus in his bosom. And he cried and said, Father Abraham, have mercy on me, and send Lazarus, that he may dip the tip of his finger in water, and cool my tongue; for I am tormented in this flame."*

The above passages prove that the result of not using life the way God designs it for is to lose it in hell. Who would have believed that a man can end up in hell for not sharing his things with others. Some, especially secular people may argue that the man is free to use his things the way he likes. The point that knocks off this argument is found in 1Timothy 6:7, which says, **"For we brought nothing into this world, and it is certain we can carry nothing out."** Everything about a man on earth is made up of borrowed or temporary items, including his body. His spirit which God gives to him to live on earth would be taken from him sooner or later. When the spirit is taken from, he begins the life in eternity in heaven or his second death in hell, according to Revelation 21:8. The Bible says in Ecclesiastes 12:7, **"Then shall the dust return to the earth as it was: and the spirit shall return unto God who gave it."** Anyone who feels that he has anything of his own does not need to wait until he dies before he knows that he is wrong. All he needs to do is to go to the mortuary and find out this truth.

When a man uses his life for these purposes, he will enjoy it to its fullness. Some people who are not even Christians enjoy life when they put smiles on the faces of others. Some even go as far as saying, *"givers never lack."* Out of all God gave to the foolish man in the Bible which include the gift of life, good health, power or wisdom to make money, the land where he sowed, the rain and the sunlight that made him to have so much harvest; God took only one which is the gift of life.

You will notice that most if not all of the things in what Dale Carnegie analyzed as human desires are omitted in biblical perspectives. The reason is that the desire to serve the Lord had covered virtually everything in the items. When a person desires to serve the Lord, many things, which he does not even ask for, naturally come to him. This explains the reason Jesus said Matthew 6:33, **"Seek ye first the kingdom of God, and his righteousness; and all these things shall be added unto you."** Quite unfortunately, most

Christians do not take cognizance of this passage nowadays. Their desires which ought to be different from the secular because they are peculiar people are not quite different from the world, which Carnegie explained above. A lot of things are responsible for this, which may include but not limited to

(1.) Ignorance of the way of God. (Hosea 4:6)
(2.) Influence of wrong friends or company (1Corinthians 15:33)
(3.) Love of or Interest in the things of the world like ungodly entertainments, pleasures in worldly life etc (1 John 2:15)

Since we cannot specifically define the desires or the background of the people we are going to handle or work with, it is better to think in terms of the general cravings of a man so as to get the maximum output of them. It is instructive to note that it is not within the power of any man to enforce the scriptural principles on anyone. Only God, as a matter of fact, can convince and convict people of their sins or selfishness. As Christians, our own part is to teach Biblical principles, not to enforce them. We are also to tolerate them even if their views differ from ours. After all, no matured Christian would claim to know all he or she knows overnight.

Christian Human Resources is handling and dealing with different categories of people, according to their levels of understanding of the scriptures or knowledge about God. When dealing with them, we must understand that we are not dealing with materials or money or animals. According Carnegie, we are dealing with creatures with logics, feelings or emotions. The knowledge, beliefs and mental states of the people will always affect their productivity. So we are going to discuss some biblical principles that must be applied when dealing or handling them.

BIBLICAL PRINCIPLES IN DEALING WITH PEOPLE

Most people, ignorant and fearful ones can perform far beyond expectations if they are given enough reasons to act. Because some self imposed obstacles or other hindrances on their ways, the people remain among the spectators instead of becoming imitators of Jesus Christ that make things happen, going about doing good. These limitations are going to be discussed in line with the biblical principles in dealing with people.

THE LIMITATIONS OF FEAR: Professor William James says an average man develop 10% of his latent mental ability. Why is this so? It is because of fear - fear of not making a fool out of oneself, fear of failure and fear of uncertainty. The Bible confirms this in 2Timothy 1:7, which says, *"**For God hath not given us the spirit of fear; but of power, and of love, and of a sound mind.**"* According to this passage, fear is a spirit that can be attributed to human distrust in God. It is opposed to the power of God, the love of God and to God-given ability of man to think and operate like a son of God. Fear is one of the greatest weapons of the enemies of Christians. With fear, a child of God whose life is threatened can be reduced into meat for the enemies to consume. With fear, a giant who is a potential terror to the host of hell can be reduced into a midget that runs from the battle. With fear, the enemies can depressed, oppressed and even possessed a person who is once a vibrant Christian. With fear, however little, a Christian cannot make exploits that is in proposition with his or her potentials. Because fear can greatly limit a Christian, God repeats it about 365 times in the Bible, *"**fear not.**"* Strange enough, there is no one without fear, however small or great. So when dealing with anyone, we must understand that by his or her nature, he or she is afraid of something. That thing can ultimately affect his or her productivity or corporation with others. A leaders does not need to know the cause of fear before he can deals with it. For unreasonable reasons, many people find it hard to share the feelings of fear. More often than not, they secretly nurse the feelings fear until they grow into monsters. As I indicated in one of my books, you empower what you fear. When you confront the thing you fear head on, you reduce the power until it becomes nothing. Christians cannot afford to let fear rule them in any way. They can use these principles to overcome fear:

(a) Confession of the weakness to the Lord in prayer (b) Studies and application of the word of God.

(c) Using the promise of God in the passage that counter the thing you fear. For instance if you are afraid of death, use the passage in Psalm 118:17 that says, *"**I shall not die, but live, and declare the works of the LORD.**"*

(d) Bold the courage to face what you fear. For instance, if you afraid to minister the word of God to people, especially those you feel are more knowledgeable than you, start ministering to children who would hardly notice you flaws. You can also start mastering what you want to teach them and then first teach your family or friends who would share their candid opinion with you instead of bringing you with their criticisms.

THE LIMITATIONS OF CRITICISMS OR NEGATIVE OPINIONS:

Because of the desire in a man to be important, criticism or negative opinion about a person can make him or her give up any attempt to make exploit, forcing him or her to be a spectator that watches things instead of imitator of God who makes things to happen. Most people do not like to be criticized for any reason because of the natural feelings that criticism exposes their weakness and reduces their importance or relevance.

Another reason people do not like to be criticized is that criticism influences others to form negative opinions about them. This invariably affects their conduct. To handle this problem in Christian Human Resource, first study Matthew 7:2-5, which says, ***"For with what judgment ye judge, ye shall be judged: and with what measure ye mete, it shall be measured to you again. And why beholdest thou the mote that is in thy brother's eye, but considerest not the beam that is in thine own eye? Or how wilt thou say to thy brother, Let me pull out the mote out of thine eye; and, behold, a beam is in thine own eye? Thou hypocrite, first cast out the beam out of thine own eye; and then shalt thou see clearly to cast out the mote out of thy brother's eye."***

The above passage can be interpreted like this: ***"with the same judgmental attitude you show to others would be shown to you: and the same measure of criticism you give to others (especially to those who are trying to make exploit for the Lord in their own little way) would be measured to you. And why should you point out the fault in the life or works of others without you thinking to the filth in your own life or works? Or why should you say to a fellow Christian (who probably is struggling to get things right with God), "let me correct your errors" whereas you are full of blunders yourself? You hypocrite, first clean your own mess so that you can be in a better position to gently correct others."***

The message in the passage is clear enough. Jesus tells everyone here that no one is in the position to criticize others without first criticizing himself. After first criticizing himself, a person can gently correct others who are not getting it right. The method of gentle correction was laid down by Jesus in John 8:3-11. The passage reads, ***"And the scribes and Pharisees brought unto him a woman taken in adultery; and when they had set her in the midst, They say unto him, Master, this woman was taken in adultery, in the very act. Now Moses in the law commanded us, that such should be stoned: but what sayest thou? This they said, tempting him, that they might have to accuse him. But Jesus stooped down,*** *and with his finger wrote on the ground, as though he heard them not. So when they continued asking him, he lifted up himself, and said unto them, He that is without sin among you, let him first cast a stone at her. And again he stooped down, and wrote on the ground. And they which heard it, being convicted by their own conscience, went out one by one, beginning at the eldest, even unto the last: and Jesus was left alone, and the woman standing in the midst. When Jesus had lifted up himself, and saw none but the woman, he said unto her, Woman, where are those thine accusers? hath no man condemned thee? She said, No man, Lord. And Jesus said unto her, Neither do I condemn thee: go, and sin no more."*

The word of God does not encourage critical or judgmental attitudes for the following reasons:

(1) Criticisms, especially destructive type can dampen or even destroy efforts of others who are trying to learn or get things right. Criticism can be so dangerous that it can kill. It made sensitive Thomas Hardy, one of finest novelists that ever enriched English literature to give up writing. Criticism drove Thomas Chatterton, the English poet to commit suicide.

(2) Criticism often times does not encourage learning. Instead of that, it sometimes makes a person feel stupid or even vengeful.

(3) More often than not, the motive behind criticism is always wrong. If a person has the right motive, he would first of all praise the efforts of others for even making attempts to perform the task. Christian Human Resource can change what looks like criticism into correction which is constructive by first praising the efforts of others before pointing out rooms for improvements.

(4) Criticism can bring about fear of negative opinions of others, thereby destroying the chances to develop self-confidence that may be required in making exploits for the Lord. Some institutes that train people in public speaking often force each student to talk at every session of the course on public speaking. Through that, the students develop courage, confidence and enthusiasm. If they are so criticized, all these can be dampened.

Criticism and fear of negative opinions of others are part of what make most people shy away from leadership roles. Most resource persons know that criticism is futile because it put a man on the defensive. It actually makes him try to justify himself. Criticism, especially destructive type is very dangerous because it wounds a man's precious pride, hurts his sense of importance and arouses his resentment. To buttress this view, I would give the case study of myself when I was still very young in Christianity. I was one of the students that were going through workers in training in the Sunday School in the Church. While going through the practical in workers in training class, I was told to prepare a lesson and teach the class. On the day I was to teach, I put on the only suit I had. I thought I had prepared a good lesson until a student who probably wanted me to realize that I still had a lot to learn criticized my lesson. He so much attacked me with criticism that I was very hurt although I hid this from everybody. Our teacher who has a lot of experience knew how the criticism must have felt like. He defended my lesson but I decided I was going to hit the student back when it was his turn to deliver his lecture. I waited for the time the student will deliver his own lecture. Of course, I criticized his lesson too. It was later that God made me realized that what I did was a great sin. I had criticized the brother with bad intension even though I thought I had criticized him constructively. Thank God, He delivered me from the sin on time.

MANAGEMENT OF CHRISTIAN HUMAN RESOURCE

The Bible says in Matthew 9:35-38, *"And Jesus went about all the cities and villages, teaching in their synagogues, and preaching the gospel of the kingdom, and healing every sickness and every disease among the people. But when he saw the multitudes, he was moved with compassion on them, because they fainted, and were scattered abroad, as sheep having no shepherd. Then saith he unto his disciples, The harvest truly is plenteous, but the labourers are few; Pray ye therefore the Lord of the harvest, that he will send forth labourers into his harvest."*

These two questions require answers before anyone can appreciate the importance of this passage: who are the labourers Jesus referred to and why are they few? To get answers there is need to study labourers in God's vineyard.

Labourers in God's vineyard: Jesus gave a graphic illustrations of labourers in God's vineyard in Mat 20:1-16 *"For the kingdom of heaven is like unto a man that is an householder, which went out early in the morning to hire labourers into his vineyard. And when he had agreed with the labourers for a penny a day, he sent them into his vineyard. And he went out about the third hour, and saw others standing idle in the marketplace, And said unto them; Go ye also into the vineyard, and whatsoever is right I will give you. And they went their way. Again he went out about the sixth and ninth hour, and did likewise. And about the eleventh hour he went out, and found others standing idle, and saith unto them, Why stand ye here all the day idle? They say unto him, Because no man hath hired us. He saith unto them, Go ye also into the vineyard; and whatsoever is right, that shall ye receive. So when even was come, the lord of the vineyard saith unto his steward, Call the labourers, and give them their hire, beginning from the last unto the first. And when they came that were hired about the eleventh hour, they received every man a penny. But when the first came, they supposed that they should have received more; and they likewise received every man a penny. And when they had received it, they murmured against the good man of the house, Saying, These last have wrought but one hour, and thou hast made them equal unto us, which have borne the burden and heat of the day. But he answered one of them, and said, Friend, I do thee no wrong: didst not thou agree with me for a penny? Take that thine is, and go thy way: I will give unto this last, even as unto thee. Is it not lawful for me to do what I will with mine own? Is thine eye evil, because I am good? So the last shall be first, and the first last: for many be called, but few chosen."*

Labourers are actually those who are called out of the world to become the followers of Jesus Christ, irrespective of the time each of them becomes born-again. Jesus said in John 15:16 ***"Ye have not chosen me, but I have chosen you, and ordained you, that ye should go and bring forth fruit, and that your fruit should remain: that whatsoever ye shall ask of the Father in my name, he may give it you."***

Note the following characteristics in God's methodology of engaging workers in His vineyard in the above passages:
1. Everybody that is saved is called to serve Jesus Christ (the good man in the parable) in God's vineyard, which is in this world.
2. Every labourer's needs in God's vineyard are always taken care of by the Lord through one way or the other.
3. It does not matter the time the labourers join in the work. All will be entitled to the same reward as the early workers.
4. God always meets all the needs of the labourers.
5. More often than not, the first comes last while the last comes first.

Let us consider the three out of common reasons the first always come last and the last comes first.

1. The amount of zeal each of labourer puts into the work will determine if he or she would remain first and relevant in the vineyard. The Bible says in Romans 12:11, *"(a Christian worker is) not slothful in business; fervent in spirit; serving the Lord…"*
2. The second reason may be found in 1 Peter 2:7-8, which says, **"Unto you therefore which believe he is precious: but unto them which be disobedient, the stone which the builders disallowed, the same is made the head of the corner, And a stone of stumbling, and a rock of offence, even to them which stumble at the word, being disobedient: whereunto also they were appointed."** This passage makes it clear that there are some labourers that have become stumbling blocks to others. Hence only those who are still obedient to the word of God are precious to the Lord. When you consider the way some ministers use the name of the Lord for commercial and other wrong purposes, you will understand the reason Jesus said in Matthew 7:22-23, **"Many will say to me in that day, Lord, Lord, have we not prophesied in thy name? and in thy name have cast out devils? and in thy name done many wonderful works? And then will I profess unto them, I never knew you: depart from me, ye that work iniquity."**
3. The other reason to consider is the intents of the heart or the motive behind the activities of the labourers. In Hebrew 4:12, the Bible says, *"For the word of God is quick, and powerful, and sharper than any two-edged sword, piercing even to the dividing asunder of soul and spirit, and of the joints and marrow, and is a discerner of the thoughts and intents of the heart."* If God sees that the motive behind the good works of a person is not in line with His word, he or she would be considered as a borrowed vessel. I know of a pastor who practically prostrated to his congregation while appealing to the people to give into the work of God. It was later discovered that almost half of what he raised as fund for the Church building project went into his pocket. It was then the people discovered the reason he went that far to appeal for fund.

Christian Human Resource management would need to put the above weakness into consideration before it can effective manage the manpower, money and material resources within the Christian organization or ministry. Once these are put into considerations, wrong person would not be placed to man right place or right person would not be placed to man the wrong job. The reason as explained earlier is that materials and money are non-living items, which had to be used by manpower. The way man uses materials or money in an organization often determines the success or failure of that organization. So manpower must be the major focus in the management in Christian Human Resources.

When we are talking about management in general, information about each of the resources is vital. Information is what manpower uses for efficient management. Information covers the aspect of manpower itself and every other thing about the organization, including the output. An efficient manager or leader needs all information he could lay his hand on before he can make good and sound judgments. So a leader or manager seeks or equips himself with information about everything he does in an organization. When a manager or leader wants to recruit someone to fill an important position in an organization, he needs some vital information about that person. Apart from that, he needs to get information about everybody in the organization in order to know his or her skills, mental abilities, loyalties e.t.c. All these will help him to understand how to deal, relate or handle or manage the people.

MANAGEMENT OF THE PEOPLE IN A CHRISTIAN ORGANIZATION

Dealing with people is the biggest problem everybody faces everywhere in the world, including the Christendom. Because nobody has the Eyes of God to see things, the leader would need to get information and understand the people, especially gifted ones who may claim to be Christians but, in truth, they are yet to know Christ. The Bible says in Jeremiah 17:9-10, *"The heart is deceitful above all things, and desperately wicked: who can know it? I the LORD search the heart, I try the reins, even to give every man according to his ways, and according to the fruit of his doings."* Of course, this does not exclude anyone. Someone who is filled with good intention today does not mean he or she cannot be influenced to be filled with bad intents the next day. So, as the first law, Christian Human Resource must not assume that it is dealing with Angels of God who can perfectly do things right. The leader in an organization must not feel betrayed or disappointed by the people he trusts if they let him down in anyway. Since human is not perfect, we all betrayed

God one way or the other just like Peter whom Jesus told Matthew 16:18, *"And I say also unto thee, That thou art Peter, and upon this rock I will build my church; and the gates of hell shall not prevail against it."* The same disciple who later became one of the greatest Apostles in the Bible betrayed Jesus in Mark 14:66-72. If someone like Peter betrayed Jesus three times and was still given the chance to be reconciled, Christian leaders MUST always create rooms for reconciliations. It may be hard but it a MUST for everybody involved in management of Christian Human Resources.

One of the hallmarks of sound Christian Human Resources is the ability to manage, tolerate and readily forgive people for whom they are and for what they have done wrong. If a leader does these, he would get the best performances of the people in spite of their weaknesses. This explains the reasons the result of an investigation conducted by an institute on successes indicated that 15% of one's financial success is due to one's technical knowledge and about 85% is due to skill in human engineering like personality and ability to lead people. John B, Rockefeller said, *"the ability to lead people is a purchase-able a commodity as sugar and coffee. And I will pay more for that ability than for any other under the sun."* Dale Carnegie said in his book titled: How to win friend and influence people, *"When dealing with people, let us remember that we are dealing with creature of logic, we are dealing with creatures of emotion, creatures bristling with prejudices and motivated by pride and vanity."*

General speaking, people can be delicate, sensitive or even dangerous to handle. A lot of people try avoid dealing with others because of what they have experienced. Some people can kill out of jealousy, anger or out of sheer love of money. There is a Nigerian case of a man who lent his friend some money. The friend did not want to pay back what he owned. So he sent hired killers to eliminate the man. Through God's intervention, the killers asked the man a few questions which brought about truths. The killers left the man without even touching him. That is to show how dangerous some people can be if they are mishandled. Mere criticism can invoke provocation or hatred or even cause trouble. Dale Carnegie said, *"if you and I want to stir up a resentment tomorrow than any rankle across the decade and endure till death, just let us indulge in a little stinging criticism, no matter how certain we are that it is justified."* We shall study some rules in dealing with people, some of which are suggested by Dale Carnegie and confirmed by the scriptures.

RULE 1: Be genuinely interested in the people. If you want people to cooperate with you in anything, especially in the management of human resources, you need to be genuinely interested in them. Many people are so interested in themselves and in what they want to get that they are never interested in others, including those that help them. The passage that confirms this in Christian Human Resources is found in Romans 12:9-10. The Bible passage says, *"Let love be without dissimulation. Abhor that which is evil; cleave to that which is good. Be kindly affectioned one to another with brotherly love; in honour preferring one another."*

RULE 2: Always put on smiles. The Chinese Proverb says: *"A man without a smiling face must not open shop."* All Christians need to show the joy of salvation through their smiles and in all the things they do. The Bible says in Isaiah 61:10, *"I will greatly rejoice in the LORD, my soul shall be joyful in my God; for he hath clothed me with the garments of salvation, he hath covered me with the robe of righteousness, as a bridegroom decketh himself with ornaments, and as a bride adorneth herself with her jewels."* I know a Christian lady who used to bring snacks to our office when I was in Nigerian Civil Service some years ago. Her snacks were not as good as others' but this sister has an outstanding quality. She was always full of smiles. There is no time we saw her without smiles. Because of this smile, she always sold all the snacks she brought while others who had better ones did not always sell half of what she sold. When the Christian sister made mistakes in making the snacks, her customers readily forgave her, saying, *"if not for those smiles, we won't buy these from you."* Christians who are serious about working with the Lord must always puts on smiles. Imagine a situation where an Evangelist with frowned face approaching a sad man and then start sharing the word of God with the sad looking man, saying, *"...the Bible says the joy of the Lord is our strength."* You would not expect the sad man to take him seriously, at least not with frowned face.

RULE 3: Remember names of the people you are dealing with. One of the simplest, most obvious and most important ways of gaining goodwill is by remembering the names of people. This always makes them feel important. Actually every soul is important and precious to God. Respect them by calling them Mr. Mrs. Or Miss or Brother or

Sister or Pastor or Evangelist etc. By doing that, you are respecting them and making them feel important. Sometimes, if you do not respect someone or make them feel important, he or she bears grudges which you cannot explain nor trace the root. They would simply refuse to cooperate with you without telling you why. The Bible says in Romans 12:10, *"Be kindly affectioned one to another with brotherly love; in honour preferring one another..."*

RULE 4: Be pitiful and courteous with people. The Bible says in 1 Peter 3:8, *"Finally, be ye all of one mind, having compassion one of another, love as brethren, be pitiful, be courteous..."* Do not be surprised if you discover that some of the people you are dealing with in Christian Human Resources are selfish. Even if they are, be sympathetic and listen to whatever they want to say. Dale Carnegie said, *"remember that the person you are talking to is a hundred times more interested in himself, his wants and problems than he is in you and your problems. His toothache means more to him than a famine that kills a million people. A boil on his neck interests him more than forty earthquakes in Africa."* You can encourage him to talk about himself and his accomplishments. Ask questions which he will readily answer. This will show that you are really interested in him or her. If you do that, you would be better equipped in the way to handle him. Besides, you can learn through him or her. It does not really matter if it is negative or positive lesson.

RULE 5: Avoid any argument. The Bible says in Proverb 18:6, *"A fool's lips enter into contention, and his mouth calleth for strokes."* The case of a Christian gentleman who was challenged by an atheist before a crowd readily comes to my mind. The gentleman who accepted the challenge to debate about the existence of God was not a public speaker. He told the people that he only want to tell the story of his conversion into Christianity, not to debate with the atheist. He was able to defeat the atheist and won the hearts of the people to Christ simply by sharing his testimony. Again Dale said, *"if you argue and rankle and contradict, you may achieve a victory sometimes, but it will be an empty victory because you will never get your opponent's good will. It is impossible to defeat an ignorant man by argument. Let your husband or wife or friend or customer or any of your listeners beat you in the little discussion that may arise... Hatred is never defeated by hatred but by love. The misunderstanding is never ended by argument but by tact, diplomacy, conciliation and a sympathetic desire to see other people's point of view. Show respect to other people's opinion. Never tell a man he is wrong, be diplomatic in dealing with people. If you feel the need to put him right in his view, begin with praise and honest appreciation."* Do not use hammer and dynamite method to prove a point. After all, no man is 100% wrong and no man in 100% correct. Definitely, the man may have a point. Help him emphasis on the point he is right about, praise it before you begin to tactically correct him. For instance you can put it this way, *"don't you think this other aspect is like this or that? Or suppose we look at this aspect like this or that."* Some twenty years ago, a man was trying to argue that fax machine works without the use of telephone lines. This argument so irritated me that I told him if he wanted to argue, he should argue about what he knew. That statement spurred him to argue the more. He wanted to save his face in the presence of other people that were round. To put an end to the argument, I brought out a business card of a newspapers editor friend, who has the same telephone number as his fax number. That ended the argument but, of course, the man never became my friend. I had disgraced him without knowing it. So you must be careful to avoid argument even though the other person is wrong. An adage says, *"arguments spoil friendships."*

RULE 6: If you are wrong, admit it quickly. It is a sign of humility. The Bible says in Proverb 15:33, *"The fear of the LORD is the instruction of wisdom; and before honour is humility."* You can even make fun of yourself if you like. People would readily forgive you for your mistakes if you quickly admit it. Instead of reducing their confidence in your leadership, the admission of error would make they increase it. According to Dale, *"any fool can try to defend his mistakes and most fools do."* Sometimes ago, I was accused of what I did not do by two of the people working with me in the Church. I was in the position to suspend them for the wrong accusation if I prove my innocence. My wife expected me to at least defend myself but I did not do that. Instead I apologized for the wrong impressions they had, telling them that my position as the lead Pastor is not meant to defend myself but to lead others in the path of righteousness. It was after then that the people confessed the truth. I won more respect and confidence of everyone.

RULE 7: Dramatize or illustrate your idea. Merely starting a truth may not enough. It must be made vivid, interesting and dramatic. Tell stories or give illustrations if you love to. Jesus used parables to explain certain things which are strange to His audience. If you really want to carry people along in your vision, you need to dramatize or illustrate your idea in a way the people would understand. If you do not do that, chances are that they won't know what to do. If it is well illustrated, the entire human resources available to you would get the picture. If they are able to catch the vision, they would cooperate and even offer suggestions on how to implement the goal or vision. Calvary Rock Resources often times uses movies and drama books to explain events of in the spirit real which people cannot perceive or imagine with human senses.

RULE 8: Challenge the people to put the idea into practice. All human beings naturally learn things by doing them. After Jesus had taught His disciples how to become fishers of men, He challenged them to go after the lost sheep in specific areas. In Matthew 10:5-7, the Bible says, **"These twelve Jesus sent forth, and commanded them, saying, Go not into the way of the Gentiles, and into any city of the Samaritans enter ye not: But go rather to the lost sheep of the house of Israel. And as ye go, preach, saying, The kingdom of heaven is at hand."** Some years ago, after teaching the children between the age of eight and twelve about preaching to adults, including their parents, I took them out into different busy areas in the city to share the word of God. I selected the ones that would lead in praises to God and the ones that would preach. I restricted them to messages about hell, heaven and sins which I have taught them. I was surprised at the way the children delivered the word of God. Of course, this inspired most of them to become preachers. Some of these children are now adult ministers.

RULE 9: Encourage the people: There is no group of people in the world who needs encouragements like Christians. The reason is that Christian life is full of struggles, battles and persecutions. For this reasons, the word of God is full of encouragements. In Hebrew 3:13, the Bible instructed, **"But exhort one another daily, while it is called To-day; lest any of you be hardened through the deceitfulness of sin."** To get maximum output in Christian Human Resources, every Christian, especially matured ones must always encourage one another. More often than not, everybody's efforts however small need to be appreciated before a Christian can be encouraged. People with critical attitudes often find it hard to praise the efforts of others. These people are usually poor leaders who hardly get followers in voluntary organizations. Instead of appreciating the good works of members of their team, some leaders keep silent or try to look for faults, thinking they want to make the work perfect. When they do any of these, they dampen or destroy the efforts of members of their teams. In Christian Human Resources, if you do not encourage good works, you naturally discourage them. Encouragement often times cost the giver nothing but gives so much to the receiver. It is so important to the receiver that if he is denied of it, his life can be changed negatively. Everybody in the world, including Christian Human Resource needs encouragement. Why not give it to one another since it does not make anyone poor but enriches those who receive it. *"Years ago,"* says Dale Carnegie, **"a young man in London aspired to be a writer but everything seemed to be against him. He had never been able to attend school for more than four years. His father been flung in jail because he couldn't pay his debts and this young man often knew the pangs of hunger. Finally, he got a job pasting labels on bottled of blacking in a rat infested warehouse, and he slept at nights in a dismal attic room with two other boys - gutter snipes from the slumps of London. He had so little confidence in his ability to write that he sneaked out and mailed his first manuscript in the dead of night to avoid ridicules. Story after story was refused until one was accepted. He wasn't paid a shilling for it but the editor had given him recognition. He was so thrilled and encouraged that he wandered aimlessly around the streets with tears rolling down his cheeks... That person is called Charles Dickens."** Coincidentally, some of the things God used to inspire me to be a writer when I was a teenager were Charles Dickens' literary works.

RULE 10: Correct errors with good intention. The Bible says in Ephesians 4:14-15, **"That we henceforth be no more children, tossed to and fro, and carried about with every wind of doctrine, by the sleight of men, and cunning craftiness, whereby they lie in wait to deceive; But speaking the truth in love, may grow up into him in all things, which is the head, even Christ:"** Because some people may be deceived by different doctrines and cunning craftiness of Christian imposters, there is need to sometimes correct errors in Christian Human Resources. To correct any error, the leader needs to use the word of God with love and good intention.

The above rules are about the major things to follow in handling people in Christian Human Resources. Dale Carnegie says something very important for all Christians to note. He said, *"the only reason why you are not a rattle snake is because your parents are not rattlesnakes. The only reason you don't kiss a cow or consider snake holy is because you were not born into Hindu family or banks of Brahmaputra. So you deserve little or no credit for what you are."* The passage that confirms this truth is found in Galatians 2:16, which says, *"Knowing that a man is not justified by the works of the law, but by the faith of Jesus Christ, even we have believed in Jesus Christ, that we might be justified by the faith of Christ, and not by the works of the law: for by the works of the law shall no flesh be justified."*

The above passage helps all Christians to grab the fact that they are justified only by faith in Jesus, not by works. Thus it must be noted that the reason a person behaves in an ungodly way is due to his or her ignorance of the word of God. Similarly, some Christians may still act in sinful ways because of their immaturity in the spirit. Just as you cannot punish a baby for defecating on the bed, you cannot condemn a babe Christian who still behaves like a sinner. What you need to do is to nurture the babe Christians with the word of God until they are matured enough to know what are expected of them. That was what Jesus did to virtually all His disciples, including Peter.

UNDERSTANDING THE MANAGEMENT OF CHRISTIAN HUMAN RESOURCES

As explained while talking about dealing with people, human beings are not robots that can be programmed but emotional and logical people. They are so complicated that each of them needs to be studied individually before they can be effectively handled. While some have to be appealed to logically, some can be carried along with simple jokes. Some have to be treated like very important person before you can get the best from them.

In management of people, the following must be understood and followed:
(1) People need to be studied individually. They need to be understood before they can be well handled or managed.
(2) Understand their abilities. As everybody is created by God with different abilities, their temperaments; physical, emotional and spiritual capasities must be carefully studied. A person might not

know his ability until somebody else points it out to him. Prof. William James said, *"... Man possesses power of various sorts which he habitually fails to use."*

(3) Try to understand or visualize the result of the assignment you are giving to the person, based on previous assignments or his records. That may be important in choosing the right person for the job. For instance, while trying to assign roles to casts in one of our movies, I watched the previous film where the potential of a good Christian actor had been underutilized. Based on his performance in only one scene, I was able to visualize he must be good. So I assigned him a major role. Of course, he performed very well.

(4) Work on the willingness of the people to accept responsibility. Study the rules on how to deal with human beings in the previous lessons. The willingness of an unskilled person to perform a job may turn out to be better than the unwillingness of a skilled person who is forced to perform the same job.

(5) Reliability in a person is important. A person may have all the abilities to perform a job but if he is unreliable, he may not be fit for the job.

ORGANIZATIONAL STRUCTURE

Every organization must be well organized before it can effectively carry out its aims and objectives. To get any organization organized, there must be organizational arrangement (structure). The framework which allows flows of power to subordinate bodies may be referred to as organizational structure. For instance, the manager of a company has subordinates that are accountable to him. The manager is may also be accountable to somebody. The flow of power or authority goes on like that till it reaches the chairman of the board or the President. Similar thing is applicable in Christian Human Resource as indicated in Romans 13:1-2. The passage says, **"Let every soul be subject unto the higher powers. For there is no power but of God: the powers that be are ordained of God. Whosoever therefore resisteth the power, resisteth the ordinance of God: and they that resist shall receive to themselves damnation."**

For the reason of flow of power, every organization, including Church and other ministries needs an authority structure that indicates who is accountable to who. Another purpose for the structure is to indicate sections, according to the functions of the organization. The bigger the organization, the broader the authority structure. Often times, there are conflicts of powers and functions within if the job descriptions of workers or areas of jurisdictions or limitations of various authorities within the organizations are not well defined or specified. So it is important to first define the aims and objectives of the entire organization before it can be structured and divided into sections or departments.

AIMS AND OBJECTIVES OF AN ORGANIZATION

The aims and objectives will determine how the workers within an organization would function. The functions of workers would determine the division of labour. The division of labour would determine the various sections. Of course, the sections would determine the structure of the organization.

The aims and objectives which can be regarded as goals and visions of a ministries in Christian Human Resources serve as a map that would take the organization from one level to another.

Defining the aims and objectives of an organization cannot be compromised with for the following though not limited to these reasons:

(1) Without aims and objectives, all the three resources - manpower, money and materials could be wasted or exhausted without achieving anything. This can cause the organization to either fold up or go into bankruptcy. In Christian Human Resources, the end result of not having a vision is to destroy the potentials to succeed in the ministries, including success of journey to eternity in heaven. In Proverb 29:18 *"Where there is no vision, the people perish: but he that keepeth the law, happy is he."* This passage proves to every Christian that God takes the issue of visions very seriously.

(2) Aims and objectives are vital in making sound decisions and judgment because they are things that give people within organizations insights of what to do and how to do it. Without them, the workers work and walk like blind people who do not know where they are going or where they are coming from. In Isaiah 59:10-11, the Bible says of the people of God, *"We grope for the wall like the blind, and we grope as if we had no eyes: we stumble at noonday as in the night; we are in desolate places as dead men. We roar all like bears, and mourn sore like doves: we look for judgment, but there is none; for salvation, but it is far off from us."*

(3) Finally, without aims and objectives, the leader would not have

any visions to share with his or her team nor understand how to recruit, educate, motivate and navigate members. In Habakkuk 2:2-3, the Bible says, *"And the LORD answered me, and said, Write the vision, and make it plain upon tables, that he may run that readeth it. For the vision is yet for an appointed time, but at the end it shall speak, and not lie: though it tarry, wait for it; because it will surely come, it will not tarry."* This passage plainly proves that the aims and objectives in Christian Human Resources are so vital that they must be written down for people to study. It is instructive to note that a visionary may not necessarily be the one that would carry out the visions he or she receives from God. There are many cases that prove this truth in the Bible and in this generation.

Every organization has reasons for its existence. So it is necessary to spell out its aims and objectives in order to direct all the machineries towards that purposes. Anybody that is working against the purpose can be considered as a threat to the progress or survival of the organization. Similarly any ineffective or lazy worker can easily cripple the organization.

While defining the aims and objectives of the organization, it is also important to spell out the principles or regulations in the code of conduct that will guide and regulate the conduct or correct misconduct of the people involved. Naturally, people can become lawless if they are given the rooms to misbehave. The rules and regulations will check and balance their conduct. For instance, a member of an organization may decide to obtain a loan without paying it back if there is no sanction or regulation that indicates that such loan will be deducted from his salary. Also a manager may decide to dismiss a female member of the company just because she did not yield to his lustful approach. He may go away with it if there is no regulation to put his own conduct into a check.

Just as the law states, it must always be assumed that a person who is accused of misconduct in an organization is innocent unless proved otherwise. Sometimes, it is necessary to set up an ad-hoc committee to investigate an offence before proper action is taken, based on code of conduct or regulations. There are some people who need to be handled with iron hand even in Christian Human Resources so as to discourage an act. In 1 Timothy 5:18-20, the Bible says, *"For the scripture saith, Thou shalt not muzzle the ox that treadeth out the corn. And, The labourer is worthy of his reward.*

Against an elder receive not an accusation, but before two or three witnesses. Them that sin rebuke before all, that others also may fear."

If leaders must effectively lead, they must bear it in mind that most members of their teams or organization do not want to obey them unless they are given good reason to obey them. The reason may come in the form of rebuke, sanctions or even punishments. And this leads us to another aspect of human resources called "discipline."

DISCIPLINE: Can be defined as an administrative way of checking or regulating the conduct or misconduct of a person through sanction or other form of punishment in order to improve the act of an erring member of an organization or team. It can also be a way of subjecting employees to the norms or regulations of the organization in order to effectively carry out their official duties. Discipline is very vital in every organization or team for effective and smooth running of all its machineries. Without discipline, members of an organization may misbehave and also negatively influence others if they go away with their offences. The misconduct will invariably affect productivity of manpower resources. It may come as a surprise that there are lots of Christians who do not know that they steal from their employer by spending the office hours to do personal things. They justify their actions by giving excuses without thinking that their employers are paying for the working hours, which they use for personal things.

In Proverb 15:10, the Bible says, *"Correction is grievous unto him that forsaketh the way: and he that hateth reproof shall die."* Here we can see that if discipline is not enforced in Christian Human Resources, it can lead to problems, including death. An organization whose members are not disciplined will destroy every potential to grow or to carry out its aims and objectives. Discipline can be used to control excessive freedom. It is therefore necessary to spell out the consequences of every offence or unscrupulous acts in the form of regulations. These regulations can be used to discipline every erring member in an organization.

REGULATIONS: This is the laid down rules that are guiding the activities of members of an organization. The obligations, responsibilities, consequences of misconducts, rights and benefits of a member or employee are usually spelt out it. In order to effectively regulate the conduct of every member or employee in an organization, including the leader and the subordinate, there must be a regulation.

LEADERSHIP AND MANAGEMENT

The performance of members or employees of an organization will largely determine the outputs in terms of quality productions and services. How members are handled will determine their performances. A good leader always seeks for the best and creative way of improving the performances of members or employees in an organization. As earlier mentioned, human beings are not machines or robots you can manipulate. You cannot control them without appealing to their sense of reasoning, emotions or feelings. As leaders expect to get the best from members of their teams, members also expect to get the best from their leaders. Their expectations, says Lawrence Darmani in Interlit magazine, critically affect their performances.

Let us first critically examine what Lawrence Darmani observed as the expectations of staff and members within an organization which may also be applicable in Christian Human Resources.

REMUNERATION: Literally, when you hire a farm hand, his performance is determined by the quality of the food you provide at the farm for him. It is true in all forms of employment. Good remuneration i.e. salaries and other incentives attract the best employees. Graduates expect to receive salaries that commensurate with their degrees and hard work, although in developing countries like Nigeria, the economy makes this aspect difficult to do. Richard Crabbed, the manager of African Christian Press alluded to this shortfall when he said hard working staffs are not usually paid as much as they deserve.

In general study of human resources, remuneration issues are top on the list of expectations with which their employees join or abandon one organization for other. When considering remunerations, you must:

(i) Be realistic. If for the same work you pay an experienced graduate is the same amount you pay a novice, you might soon face disgruntled employees.

(ii) Communicate your limitations to all members of your team or organization. Many people are willing to accept lower salaries if they are made to see the organizations financial limitations. This is especially true where the working environment includes

recognition, respect and good relationship.
(iii) Make good on the promises made during lean season. To say, *"we'll raise salaries when things improve"* and then fail to keep the promise easily makes the staff to lose faith in the organization.

RECOGNITION: An applicant was asked by his intending employer why he wanted to leave his current place of employment. The first reason he gave was lack of recognition. For many people, respect and recognition are more critical to them than remuneration. The applicant that was seeking for recognition accepted an offer of a relatively low salary with a promise of better recognition for his qualifications and input. Some employees or members take pride in helping to build an organization and there are many ways to recognize their efforts. Some managers grant awards as a strategic way to recognize key staffs. Others grant needed holidays. Others openly or publicly show appreciations for their efforts. For others, a simple *"thank you"* goes a long way. Others use the methods of pasting the name of the best workers for the month on the notice board with or without incentives. This is a great source of motivation.

JOB SECURITY: It is always wise to make employer feel secured in their jobs otherwise, they may not be motivated to put in their best. When an employee is always threatened by the idea that he might lose his or her job, he tends to look elsewhere for another job instead of concentrating on the one he has. There is need therefore to make employees, especially good ones feel secured in their jobs for maximum output.

In conclusion, there is need to point out the fact that Christian Human Resources involves creativity. There is need, therefore, to make innovations in the job. The system must give room for changes and must welcome innovative ideas. More often than not, the people in an organization determined the way they should be coordinated. While some need to be carried along with sense of humour, some may need a lot discipline before they can put the interest of the organization into considerations. Therefore, as a general rule, there is no rigid way of coordinating people

I trust that God will help and teach you in how to manage human beings.

<u>ASSESSMENT QUESTIONS</u>

1. What do you understand by Christian Human Resources?
2. Compare and contrast human desires as explained by Dale Carnegie with the order of desires in Christian Human Resources, using Bible quotations to support your answers.
3. What are the limitations that can make people spectators instead of imitators of Jesus Christ that make things happen?
4. Explain (a) Labourers in God's vineyard (b) God's methodology of engaging workers in His vineyard (c) Reasons first set of workers sometimes comes last.
5. Explain the rules that can be applied when dealing with people.
6. Write notes on (a) The Management in Christian Human Resources (b) Organizational Structure (c) Aims And Objectives Of An Organization.
7. Explain the role of leadership in management of an organization.

CHILDREN EVANGELISM

BOOK FIVE

INTRODUCTION:

In all the ministries on earth, children evangelism is the most crucial of them all yet it is the most neglected. One of the reasons is the fact that Children evangelism does not yield immediate results. It sometimes takes so many years before the harvest comes. In most cases, the children ministers do not benefit directly from the souls they had won for Christ. Unlike in evangelization of adults, which immediately yield results as soon as the souls are converted to Christ, children evangelism takes so much effort, time and tasks the scare financial resources without yielding enough dividends to justify the investments. That is why a lot of people do not get involved in it. Even those who operate the ministry rely so much on adults to give into the work. It is very difficult, if not impossible for this type of ministry to stand on its own. Even if there are anything like children Churches it must be operated by a adult Churches that believe that children are truly the future of every society, ministries or organization. Also, it is very rare if not unrealistic to have an open-air crusade for children because of the financial implication and or other problems attached with these ministries.

Another reason, which makes this ministry very tough to operate, is that it is very difficult to minister or to get the attention of children. The ministry had to be operated by a specially trained or gifted person. Unlike in schools, one cannot beat a stubborn child anyhow. If he does that the child minister will either get the attention of the parents who are probably yet to know Christ or the child may simply stop coming to the church. With this brief introduction of this course, we shall treat children evangelism as exhaustive as time can permit us.

WHO ARE THE CHILDREN?

There is no way we can possibly understand who to call children in this context unless we look at it in the biblical point of view. Since we are treating children evangelism, we would have to find the definition of children in the Bible. Psalms 78:6 says, **"... That the generation to come might know them, even the children which should be born; who should arise and declare them to their children..."** Thus we can say the word of God define children as: the human lives that are yet to come into existence, the ones existing in the wombs, the ones at infant age and the ones that are yet to mature into adults.

Again, from the above definition, we shall see three categories of children which include the ones that are not yet to exist, the ones in the formation stage and the ones that are already born. This could be a little confusing, especially if we ask why children that are yet to exist are to be regarded as children. The simple explanation that can be offered in this regard is in the book of Genesis 1:27 and 28 where God told man to multiply. God did not create billions of people at a go. He created a couple and said to himself: *"I have created enough to make billions."* It will sound strange to us if we had been around to hear God saying to two people to take dominion over several billions of creatures on earth. In other words, God looks into those two people and saw billions of people that have never existed coming out of them.

Another illustration I will like to borrow to buttress this point is in what Myles Munroe said about potentials in a seed. He said, if I hold a seed in my hand and ask you what I am holding in my hands, your likely answer will be: a seed. That is true but not a fact. The fact is: I am holding a forest in my hand. A seed will become a tree and then brings more seeds. The seeds will grow into many trees and produce more seeds until you eventually get a forest. That is exactly the case with human beings.

To properly understand who can be called children, I would like to explain each and every category of children mentioned above.

CHILDREN THAT ARE YET TO EXIST

Children that are not yet born are as real as real as the ones that exist now, going by the passage in Psalms 78:6. Just because adults do not see the children that would be born in future does not mean that they are not real. While some of them would be born in a year's time, some in two, three, ten till kingdom. If God in mindful of the children that are yet to exist, every Christian must be mindful of them too. If God plans for them, every adult must also plan for them. The ministry of children is saddled with the responsibilities to consider future children just as teachers, ministers, parents and other adults must be conscious of the fact that a time would come when there would be lots of children that would bring forth more children into the world. This is fact of life. In a 54:1-3, the word of God says to people who are probably influenced by their present conditions to make plans that are greater than what they can perceive, *"Sing, O barren, thou that didst not bear; break forth into singing, and cry aloud, thou that didst not travail with child: for more are the children of the desolate than the children of the married wife, saith the LORD. Enlarge the place of thy tent, and let them stretch forth the curtains of thine habitations: spare not, lengthen thy cords, and strengthen thy stakes; For thou shalt break forth on the right hand and on the left; and thy seed shall inherit the Gentiles, and make the desolate cities to be inhabited."*

One of the greatest problems the nation and the world encounter is lack of vision for the children that are not yet in existence. The Bible says in Proverb 29:18, *"Where there is no vision, the people perish: but he that keepeth the law, happy is he."* In other words, God's people, including children can perish for lack of vision. If there is no vision for the children that are coming, they may perish physically or spiritually or morally or in one way or the other. Whether we like it or not, whether we know it or not, more children are coming into the world because people will never stop forming babies either legitimately or illegitimately. So the nation or the world will continue to have problem because, as we are studying now, both married and unmarried people are coming together to form lots of children. It is difficult, if not impossible to predict the member of children that will be born in a year.

There is need to put into consideration children that are yet to exist when planning for the future. We all pray to see our children's children. The question is: what is our vision for these children's children? With the rate by which young ones who are still children are turning into mothers and fathers, the chances of having so many children within a short time is very enormous.

CHILDREN IN THE FORMATION STAGE

Children in the formation stage imply the stage of pregnancy of woman. When we see a woman who is heavy with pregnancy, we must realize that she is carrying a whole generation. The normal formation stage of any child in the womb of his/her mother is nine months. In other words, a child can be brought into existence within a year. So many times, children had been terminated at this stage because it is either considered unwanted or a mistake. It must be noted here that any woman that terminates her pregnancy has committed murder as far as God is concerned. Once a child starts existing in the womb, he or she is as good as living person. In some part of the world, abortion is not illegal. There are two schools of thoughts, debating whether abortion should be made illegal or not. They are called pro-life and pro-abortion. The argument of pro-life is very powerful, creating the chances to make abortion illegal. Unless the life of the child posses a serious threat to the life of the mother, everybody including the unborn baby have the right to live, irrespective of other reasons. To the pro-abortion, children in the formation stage are not yet human beings. Their definition of human beings is someone who is already out of the womb of his mother. The question is what do you called the child in the womb? Animal embryo? The world is blind to many things about God. People look for reasons to oppose the law of God. When a woman terminates her pregnancy, she not only breaks the law of God but also deny the world purpose of that child that may be precious to other people. We can imagine what would have happened if people that invented things like electricity, airplane and others had been terminated when they were in the womb of their mothers, the world would probably be in stone age. For this and other reasons, children must not be denied of existence when they are at formation stage.

CHILDREN THAT ARE BORN

A woman made a remark which sounds quite strange but bearing some hard truths. She said after looking seriously into the great problems of the world, "when a child is born, we are supposed to weep for him or her. When a person dies, we must rejoice with him or her." She has a very good reason to say that but it is not enough to put as a defense for the decadence of the world. The real truth is: children can blessings to life. God did not plan any life to be a problem to others nor to pose threats to other life. When people use their lives to please God, sharing them with one another, they will enjoy it. In Psalm 128: 1-6, the Bible says, *"Blessed is every one that feareth the LORD; that walketh in his ways. For thou shalt eat the labour of thine hands: happy shalt thou be, and it shall be well with thee. Thy wife shall be as a fruitful vine by the sides of thine house: thy children like olive plants round about thy table. Behold, that thus shall the man be blessed that feareth the LORD. The LORD shall bless thee out of Zion: and thou shalt see the good of Jerusalem all the days of thy life. Yea, thou shalt see thy children's children, and peace upon Israel."*

Children can be blessings to the family, to the community and to the world or can constitute threats if their parents who happen to their first teachers do not train them.

GENERAL WAYS OF TEACHING A CHILD FROM INFANT

The Bible says in Proverb 22:6, Proverb 22:6 *"Train up a child in the way he should go: and when he is old, he will not depart from it."* In other words, whatever a child becomes in life depends on how he or she is trained. God does not give parents thieves or prostitutes at birth but the society, starting from parents, their first teachers who begin to mold them through three ways which are as follows:

1. ***The Godly Way***: The Bible says in Proverb 20:7, ***"The just man walketh in his integrity: his children are blessed after him."*** The godly ways of just parents are through:

- (a) **Godly Conduct:** This is done through what parents do, leading them by example in a godly manner. If parents always show love of God to everybody, the children will naturally learn the language of love through their conduct. If however they are constantly fighting, the children would learn how to fight.
- (b) **Godly Communications:** This is done through what parents say in the presence of their children. If they are always saying the right thing, they would learn to say the right thing. If they use foul language, the children simply follow suit.
- (c) **Prayers:** This aspect is the invitation to God do to His part after parents have done their parts. If God is not invited to do His part by praying for the children, efforts of parents to train up their children in the way of the Lord would amount to nothing. Thus parents must always pray and prophesy good things into their children's lives. 1 Thessalonians 5:17 says, ***"Pray without ceasing."***

2. **Negligent Way:** The Bible says in Jeremiah 31:29, ***"In those days they shall say no more, The fathers have eaten a sour grape, and the children's teeth are set on edge."*** The negligent way of teaching or training children is so common from generation to another that telling people this way is wrong would prove to be difficult. The reason is that this is the way most parents are brought up. The negligent way ranges from generation to another. In the passage, the Bible makes us to understand that the "children's teeth are set on edge" because of the negligent ways of parents, making the children to learn the negligent way they would also teach their own children too when they become parents. Just as the above, the negligent ways are as follows:

- (a) **Negligent Conduct:** A good example of the negligent conduct is the case of Eli's children who were brought up in a negligent way. This is found in 1 Samuel 2:22-25. In this case, Eli did not train up his children properly until it was too late.
- (b) **Negligent Communications:** In Jeremiah 7:26, God said to His people, ***"Yet they hearkened not unto me, nor inclined their ear, but hardened their neck: they did worse than their fathers."*** Because the older generation fail to communicate the word of God to the people of Israel, they did

worse things, which would also be communicated to their own children. Evils are being communicated to the people everyday through music and other means of communications. Many Christian parents do not border about the unchristian ways of life of their children have learnt through corrupt communication. Whereas the Bible says in 1Corinthians 15:33, "Be not deceived: evil communications corrupt good manners."

(c) **Lack Of Time To Teach And Pray For The Children:** If Paul can say of the children in Galatians 4:19, ***"My little children, of whom I travail in birth again until Christ be formed in you,"*** every Christian must also travail in birth until Christ is formed in children. Lack of care for children is very rampant among parents all over the world, including Christians probably because their own parents never cared for them when they were young.

3. <u>Ungodly Way:</u> The Bible says in Isaiah 3:12, Isaiah 3:12, ***"As for my people, children are their oppressors, and women rule over them. O my people, they which lead thee cause thee to err, and destroy the way of thy paths."*** From this passage, we can assume that the children that oppress people are trained in an ungodly way by their parents, especially mothers. Mothers of these ungodly people breed them to become ungodly when they were young. At least these mothers exercise control over them when they were young until they become ungodly people. The same process of breeding godly children is the way ungodly ones. They are:

(a) **Ungodly Conduct:** The Bible says of the children of Israel in Jeremiah 7:18, ***"The children gather wood, and the fathers kindle the fire, and the women knead their dough, to make cakes to the queen of heaven, and to pour out drink offerings unto other gods, that they may provoke me to anger."*** Here in this passage, children are taught of the way to worship idol through conduct. Idolatry has taken a different turn in modern days. It has become the worship of money and even human beings. The way some adults seek for money at the expense of their soul is mind bulging. Children watch the adults, especially their parents worshiping money that takes the form of idol and some film and music stars who sometimes call themselves with the names of God. They dance to the tune of ungodly music, thinking they are enjoying themselves without filling they are actually worship the gods of this world.

(b) **Ungodly Communications:** There are the kinds of dialogues that are directly or indirectly against the word of God. The spirits of anti-Christ had been working to corrupt human communications. Some foul languages are found their way into the entertainment industries. Some songs are filled with subliminal messages that are meant to deceive and lure people from the righteous way of life. There are so common that you will find them even right in the Church.

(c) *Curses:* Instead Of Prayers: Many adults are so ignorant that they curse their future by their children without knowing it. They feel since they do not mean what they say, it does not really matter but I tell the devil does not care if they mean what they say or not. In James 3: 5-10, the Bible says, ***"Even so the tongue is a little member, and boasteth great things. Behold, how great a matter a little fire kindleth! And the tongue is a fire, a world of iniquity: so is the tongue among our members, that it defileth the whole body, and setteth on fire the course of nature; and it is set on fire of hell. For every kind of beasts, and of birds, and of serpents, and of things in the sea, is tamed, and hath been tamed of mankind: But the tongue can no man tame; it is an unruly evil, full of deadly poison. Therewith bless we God, even the Father; and therewith curse we men, which are made after the similitude of God. Out of the same mouth proceedeth blessing and cursing. My brethren, these things ought not so to be."*** This passage is a proof that people are misusing and even teaching their children to misuse the power in their tongues.

THE PSYCHOLOGY OF A CHILD

Indeed, the world is full of much problem. Still people must come and live in it until Kingdom come.

Children are surrounded with much problem just like adults. What makes the problem so confusing for them is that their limited sense of interpretation of the problems. They see things happening. They do not know what is happening, why things are happening nor understand who or what is behind the happening. So they ask a lot of questions in other to feel comfortable with the situations. Children want to know why they have to go to school where teachers are free to discipline them. They want to know how mosquitoes can bite them when they do not have mouths. They want to why their parents have to leave them at home and go to work. They want to know what is happening to them when they are sleeping. They want to know so many things because everything is strange to them. Parents must not shun their children when they ask questions. They must try to answer every question in the way they can understand without corrupting their innocent minds. If parents shun their inquisitive children, they will go into the world and get wrong answer the head-throbbing questions. Do not be surprised if good children turn bad overnight. This may be due to the negative influence from the outside or through the wrong answers they get to the questions that border them. I remember a child in my wife's school, asking me what his parents were doing when they were on top of each other. He asked, 'are they fighting?' I have to tell the child that they were playing. We are still going to talk about how children gather influence.

The future of the children is usually determined by their parents. A child can grow into a responsible adult or an irresponsible adult years later. An irresponsible adult will later become an irresponsible parent. Naturally, the irresponsible parent will influence his or her children to become irresponsible. An irresponsible family will naturally bring about irresponsible citizens in the society. It is a chain reaction because all generations are linked together with family cord. The major cause of all the problems in Nigeria is not attributed to economic or political set up. If we think it is the economy or politics, how do we explain the causes of cultism on campuses? How do we explain the fraudulent practices of many people living in the country with good and stable economic and political environment? The truth is: charity begins at home - the family. When God gives parents children, He did not give us armed robbers or prostitute or a cultist. God gives us a child to make anything we want out of him or her. It is like God gives us a blank tape and ask us to record whatever we want on it. But because some parents are cult members themselves, their children are influenced to become cultists in the school. Because some mothers jumped from one man to another, their children too become prostitutes too.

A woman once complained to me that her daughter is running after men in the street. I told her she made her daughter what she is. She looked rather confused but I explained what meant to her by pointing out the number of men she herself had flirt around with. Children can easily give out their unscrupulous parents through what they exhibit outside the home. The way some children pray during the Sunday school or school hour sometimes indicates that their parents pray at home. Likewise, the type of things like the use of foul language exhibited by children indicate how their parents talk at home. A typical example is the case of a child who said his mother's name is bastard and his father's name is idiot. This indicated that his parents are use to calling each other names.

CLASSIFICATION OF CHILDREN

Children can be categorized into different types, depending on the issue we are dealing with. In some academic environment, children may be categorized into: the fast learner, slow learner and special learner. A professional teacher will never agree that there is a child called dullard. My experience with children proves this to be very correct. In fact, Herber S. Terrace, a psychologist proves it in a remarkable experiment that a chimpanzee could learn sign language. His book titled "NIM" was a first class evidence that chimpanzee could be made to think, communicate and even behave like humans beings. If an animal with far less inferior brain can be trained in such a way, then every normal human being can be made brilliant if not a genius unless a child is mentally sick. I am a testimony to that.

The classification of children in this case is not for the purpose of academics but for the purpose of understanding the temperaments of a child so as to know how to handle them. Since children are adults in the making, it is ideal to study the four human temperaments by Dr D. W. Ekstrand. These may be applicable to every human, including children.

THE FOUR HUMAN TEMPERAMENTS
By Dr. D. W. Ekstrand

Version of this Study: There are "reasons" for everything we do as human beings, though it is often difficult for us to understand why we think like we think, feel like we feel, or act like we act in life. Many of the answers for human behavior can be found in people's temperaments or personalities. The study of the human personality goes all the way back to the famous Greek physician Hippocrates (460-370 BC), the "father of medicine" he was born during the prophetic ministries of Nehemiah and Malachi, or some 450 years before the birth of Christ. Hippocrates' work has been researched extensively and is used as a dynamic diagnostic tool in both psychology and psychiatry to this day. A generic explanation of human "Temperaments" or "Personalities" is that all of us have been born with genetically inherited "behavioral tendencies" that are as much a part of our DNA as is the color of our hair; all of us are made up of DNA combinations passed on to us through our parents and ancestors. This fact is important because it helps us to more fully understand our basic behavioral disposition. Even though much of our human personality is inherited, it should also be noted, much of it has also been influenced and shaped by our unique environments. Most scientific research on human behavior suggests that about 50% of the variations in human personality are determined by genetic factors so our human behavior is shaped equally by our environment and by our DNA. Thus, all of us as human beings have been hard-wired by our Creator (we are not just products of random chance Ps 119:73; 139:13-16; Is 44:24), and we have all been impacted by the world around us. Furthermore, according to the scientific analysis all human personalities are commonly divided up into four major categories (with the exception of those with severe mental disorders), and these four types are further broken down into two categories Extroverts and Introverts:

Extroverted Personalities: The Choleric and Sanguine personality-types are more "out-going," more sociable, and more comfortable in a crowd, even standing out in a crowd.

Introverted Personalities: The Melancholy and Phlegmatic personality-types are more shy and "reserved" and feel anxious about being in crowd, especially at being singled-out in a crowd.

It should be noted that all human beings have a degree of each of these four personality types within them, though each person will definitely test out higher in one, with another being a close second. No individual only possesses one personality type, and most of us have a very strong secondary temperament. Should you take one of the personality tests available today, you would discover that you possess dominant characteristics in a couple of the temperaments, and each kind of personality has a general characteristic associated with it. It should be noted that there are varying degrees of Extroversion and Introversion in other words, some Phlegmatics and Melancholies "border" on being out-going, and some Cholerics and Sanguines "border" on being shy. Though the characteristics may not be true for everyone with a particular personality, they are generally true for the vast majority of people. All four personality types have general strengths and weaknesses with which people must contend, and no one personality type is better than any other. All four have both good and bad qualities, and all four are needed to make this world a better place. Whatever your temperament or personality, God is the one who has given you the abilities and sensitivities that you possess, and He has given those things to you for a purpose that you might faithfully work at developing them and using them in His service. Though our temperaments have been tainted by sin and the fall, God's Spirit is mightily at work in us transforming us into the image of Christ that we might be more effective workmen in His Kingdom (Jn 17:17-20; 2 Cor 3:18; 5:20; Eph 4:7-16; Phil 2:13). Remember, no two people are alike we are all unique and we have all been given a unique call-ing in life. Therefore it is important that we not covet qualities we do not possess; rather, that we focus on discovering God's will for our lives and enjoy serving Him with the skill-set with which we have been blessed; knowing that God wants to use us to do the work for which He designed us. So identify your skills and strengths and get to work! (Prayerfully reflect upon the following passages - Mt 6:33; 13:12; 25:14-30; Lk 12:48; Jn 21:20-22; 1 Cor 4:2; 12:4-7, 21-24; Eph 2:10).

Of all the relationships we have in life, marriage is by far the most important. A good relation-ship between a husband and a wife makes for a happy home. A marriage shadowed by bitterness, fighting and other unpleasantness leaves its scars on not only the couple, but also on their children and those around them. Good marriages are not just accidents they are the result of hard work and understanding. In general, marriages between two people with the "same personality type" have the greatest potential for clashing, and anyone married to a sanguine or choleric is in for a challenge; this is mainly due to the tendencies of these two personality types to require excessive attention and control, respectively. Thus pretty much all marriages will have fairly significant challenges. Most often "opposites do attract" Sanguine individuals tend to marry Melancholy ones, and Cholerics favor Phlegmatics; though such situations are not always the case, they do appear to be the most common. It should be noted that there is no such thing as "the ideal combination;" we are all fallen human beings with foibles and shortcomings.

Following is a brief description of each of the four temperaments or personalities at the end of each description I have listed the two primary characteristics for that temperament. By identify-ing the two temperaments that best describe who you are as a person, you should be able to identify your "strongest characteristic" be it predominantly extroversion, introversion, organizational, or relational. Aside from the Extrovert-Introvert continuum that was described above on the pre-vious page, there is the Organizational-Relational continuum Cholerics and Melancholies are more "organizational," whereas the Sanguines and Phlegmatics are more "relational." With that said, let's look at a description of the four temperaments, beginning with the "sanguine"

A. SANGUINE: The Sanguine temperament is fundamentally impulsive and pleasure-seeking. Sanguine's are frequently referred to as "the talker." They are expressive in personality... desire influence, and being enthusiastic with people... in expressing thoughts with excitement... and being the center of attention. The Sanguine is sociable and charismatic, generally warm-hearted, pleasant, lively, optimistic, creative, compassionate, and outgoing; he is the life of the party, humorous, enthusiastic, and cheerful; he easily attracts others and makes friends; he inspires others to work and join in the fun. He is sincere at heart, always a child, creative and colorful, possesses energy and enthusiasm, loves people, is a great volunteer, thrives on compliments, and doesn't hold grudges. The Sanguine likes to talk a lot... struggles with completing tasks... is chronically late... and tends to forget his obligations... he bases his decisions primarily on feelings. Sanguine types can be great parents, because they love to have fun; but their homes are often frenzied and disorganized, and the only time you find everyone silent is when they are sleeping! Sanguine people usually possess high amounts of energy, so they often seem restless and spon-taneous. This type of personality loves the life of luxury and impressing others... they are big spenders... they love to travel the world and indulge in rich, comfortable living... and they will do almost anything to satisfy their always present need to be absorbed by something meaningful and exciting. They are impulsive and often find it difficult to control their cravings; as such, people with this temperament are more susceptible to smoking, alcohol, drugs, gambling and taking risk; sadly, they are most susceptible to chemical imbalances, addictions and mood disorders. These people feel bored if they are not absorbed by something intriguing and adventurous. The Sanguine is very poor at tolerating boredom; for the most part he will try to avoid monotony and that which is routine at all costs; routine jobs and boring companions annoy him and irritate him. The Bible characters that seem to best fit the characteristics of a Sanguine are King David and Peter. In addition to the characteristics listed below, the Sanguine is essentially described as being relational and an extrovert...

Is self-composed, seldom shows signs of embarrassment, perhaps forward or bold.

Is eager to express himself before a group; likes to be heard.

Prefers group activities; work or play; not easily satisfied with individual projects.

Is not insistent upon acceptance of his ideas or plans; compliant and yielding.

Is good in details; prefers activities requiring pep and energy. Is impetuous and impulsive; his decisions are often (usually) wrong. Is keenly alive to environment, physical and social; likes curiosity. Tends to take success for granted; is a follower; lacks initiative. Is hearty and cordial, even to strangers; forms acquaintanceship easily.

Tends to elation of spirit; not given to worry and anxiety; is carefree. Seeks wide and broad range of friendships; is not selective; not exclusive in games.

Is quick and decisive in movements; pronounced or excessive energy output.

Turns from one activity to another in rapid succession; little perseverance.

Makes adjustments easily; welcomes changes; makes the best appearance possible.

Is frank, talkative, sociable, expresses emotions readily; does not stand on ceremony.

Has frequent fluctuations of mood; tends to frequent alterations of elation and depression.

B. *CHOLERIC:* The Choleric temperament is fundamentally ambitious and leader-like. The Choleric is the strongest of the extroverted Temperaments, and is sometimes referred to as a "Type A" personality or "the doer" (or "the driver"); he is a hard driving individual known for accomplishing goals... he has a lot of aggression, energy, and/or passion, and tries to instill it in others. Dominant in personality Cholerics desire control, and are best at jobs that demand strong control and authority, and require quick decisions and instant attention. The Choleric is the most insensitive of the Temperaments; they care little for the feelings of others; feelings simply don't play into the equation for them. Most Cholerics are men, and born leaders who exude confidence; they are naturally gifted businessmen, strong willed, independent, self sufficient, they see the whole picture, organize well, insist on production, stimulate activity, thrive on opposition, are unemotional and not easily discouraged. They are decisive, must correct wrongs when they see them, and compulsively need to change things. They systematize everything, are all about independence, and do not do well in a subordinate position. They are goal oriented and have a wonderful focus as they work; they are good at math and engineering, are analytical, logical and pragmatic; and are masters at figuring things out. They are skeptical and do not trust easy; they need to investigate the facts on their own, relying on their own logic and reasoning. If they are absorbed in something, do not even bother trying to get their attention. Negatively, they are bossy, domineering, impatient, can't relax, quick tempered, easily angered, unsympathetic, enjoy arguments, too impetuous, and can dominate people of other tempera-ments, especially the Phlegmatic types. Many great charismatic military and political figures were Cholerics. They like to be in charge of everything… they are workaholics who thrive on control and want their way… they are highly independent people, and have very little respect for diplomas and other credentials. They set high standards, are diligent and hard-working, are rarely satisfied, and never give up their attempts to succeed. Choleric women are very rare, but strangely are very popular people. Cholerics have the most trouble with anger, intolerance and impatience; they want facts instead of emotions; and should you get your feelings hurt, it's your problem, not theirs. The Choleric does not have many friends (though he needs them), and he has a tendency to fall into deep sudden depression, and is much prone to mood swings. The Bible characters that seem to best fit the characteristics of a Choleric are the apostle Paul, James, Martha and Titus. In addition to the characteristics listed below, the Choleric is essentially described as being organizational and an extrovert…

Is self-composed; seldom shows embarrassment, is forward or bold.

Is eager to express himself before a group if he has some purpose in view.

Is insistent upon the acceptance of his ideas or plans; argumentative and persuasive.

Is impetuous & impulsive; plunges into situations where forethought would have deterred him.

Is self-confident and self-reliant; tends to take success for granted.

Exhibits strong initiative; tends to elation of spirit; seldom gloomy; prefers to lead.

Is very sensitive and easily hurt; reacts strongly to praise or blame.
Is not given to worry or anxiety; he is seclusive.

Is quick and decisive in movement; pronounced or excessive energy output.

Has marked tendency to persevere; does not abandon something readily regardless of success.

Is characterized by emotions not freely or spontaneously expressed, except anger.

Makes best appearance possible; perhaps conceited; may use hypocrisy, deceit, disguise.

C. _PHLEGMATIC:_ The Phlegmatic temperament is fundamentally relaxed and quiet, ranging from warmly attentive to lazily sluggish. Phlegmatics are referred to as "the watcher" they are best in positions of unity and mediation, and solid in positions that desire steadiness. The Phlegmatic is most often a female who tends to be easygoing, content with herself, calm, cool and collected, tolerant of others, well-balanced, sympathetic, kind, unassuming, keeps emotions hidden, is happily reconciled to life, not in a hurry, has many friends, avoids conflict, inoffen-sive, quiet but witty, agreeable and intuitive… though they are very peaceful, patient and adaptable, they tend to be reluctant, indecisive and a worrier. They are wonderful at gathering facts, classifying them, and seeing the relationship between them; basically, they are good at generalizing, seeing the bigger picture, and reading between the lines. They are accepting, affectionate, frequently shy, and often prefer stability to uncertainty and change. Because they are fearful, indecisive and hesitant of things in life, they have a compromising nature. Phleg-matics often worries about everything. They want to know other people's deepest feelings and strive to build intimate attachments with just about everyone in their lives. They are interested in cooperation and interpersonal harmony, and this is why they preserve their family ties and friendships. They could be described as considerate, charitable, sympathetic, trusting, warm, calm, relaxed, consistent, rational, curious, and observant this makes them good adminis-trators. Phlegmatic men and women strive for greater self-knowledge, and seek to contribute to society at large. On the negative side, they are often selfish, self-righteous, judge others easily, resist change, stay uninvolved, dampen enthusiasm, and can be passive-aggressive. In large part, the Phlegmatic temperament is deemed to be a neutral temperament. The Bible characters that seem to best fit the characteristics of a Phlegmatic are Joseph, Timothy and Barnabas. In addition to the following characteristics, the Phlegmatic is essentially described as being relational and an introvert…

Is deliberative; slow in making decisions; perhaps overcautious in

minor matters.
- Is indifferent to external affairs.
- Is reserved and distant.
- Is slow in movement.
- Has a marked tendency to persevere.
- Exhibits a constancy of mood.

D. MELANCHOLIC: The Melancholic temperament is fundamentally introverted & thoughtful. Melancholies are often referred to as "the thinker." Their analytical personality's desire caution and restraint, best at attending to details and in analyzing problems too difficult for others. They tend to be deep-thinkers and feelers who often see the negative attributes of life, rather than the good and positive things. They are self-reliant and independent and get wholly involved in what they are doing. Melancholies can be highly creative in activities such as art, literature, music, health-care and ministry, and can become preoccupied with the tragedy and cruelty in the world; they long to make a significant and lasting difference in the world. Melancholies usually have a high degree of perfectionist tendencies, especially in regards to their own lives or performance. They are serious, purposeful, analytical, musical, artistic, talented, creative, self-sacrificing, conscien-tious, idealistic, philosophical, and are genius prone. They are also very "introspective" and hold themselves to a very high standard one that can rarely be achieved. They tend to be highly organized, schedule oriented, economical, tidy, neat, detail conscious, finish what they start, like charts, graphs, figures and lists, see the problems and are able to identify creative solutions with ease. Sadly, many Melancholies are also victims of deep bouts of depression that come from great dissatisfaction, disappointment, hurtful words or events. Melancholy personalities are people who have a deep love for others, while usually holding themselves in contempt. In short, melancholies take life very seriously (too much so sometimes) and it often leaves them feeling blue, helpless or even hopeless. Because they are deeply caring people, they make great doctors, nurses, social workers, ministers, and teachers. This comes from a deep sense of what others are feeling or experiencing and the inward need to reach out and do something in order to help them. They are extremely loyal in friendships; there is an old saying that goes like this: "If you have a Melancholy for a friend, you have a friend for life." Most Melancholies have a low self-image, are inclined toward depression, think "self-promotion" is tacky, are continually into "fixing themselves," are notoriously "guilty" (they have an over-active conscious), and tend to worry much too often about their health. The Bible characters that seem to best fit the characteristics of a Melancholy are Moses and Abraham. In addition to the following characteristics listed below, the Melancholy is essentially described as being organizational and an introvert...

Is self-conscious, easily embarrassed, timid, bashful. Avoids talking before a group; when obliged to he finds it difficult.

Prefers to work and play alone. Good in details; careful. Is deliberative; slow in making decisions; perhaps overcautious even in minor matters.

Is lacking in self-confidence and initiative; compliant and yielding. Tends to detachment from environment; reserved and distant except to intimate friends.

Tends to depression; frequently moody or gloomy; very sensitive; easily hurt.

Does not form acquaintances readily; prefers narrow range of friends; somewhat exclusionary.

Worries over possible misfortune; crosses bridges before coming to them.

Is secretive; seclusive; shut in; not inclined to speak unless spoken to.

Is slow in movement; deliberative or perhaps indecisive; moods frequent and constant.

Often represents himself at a disadvantage; modest and unassuming.

Closing note to this section: The biblical characters listed above Joseph, Timothy, Barnabas, David, Peter, Paul, James, Titus, Martha, Moses, and Abraham obviously possessed temperaments other than the one attributed to them. These individuals were chosen because of the behavioral tendencies they demonstrated at various times in biblical history.

ASSESSMENT QUESTIONS

1. Explain whom the Bible says are children, supporting your answers with Bible passages.
2. Explain the children that are yet to exist within the context of Children Evangelism.
3. Write notes on(I) the children that are yet to exist (II) the children in the formation (III) children that are born within the context of Children Evangelism.

3. Write notes on stage within the context of Children Evangelism.
4. If you are giving the opportunity to preach at a naming ceremony, how would you teach the people all the ways of ot teaching a child from infant. Support all your answers with Bible passages.
5. Explain the psychology of a child.
6. According to Dr D W Ekstrand' explanations of the four human temperaments which are also divided into two, write short notes on the two temperaments in the category of extroverts.
7. 6. According to Dr D W Ekstrand's explanations of the four human temperaments which are also divided into two, write short notes on the two temperaments in the category of introverts.

CHECK OUT OTHER BOOKS BY DIPO TOBY ALAKIJA

Each Serves Either As Edifying Or Evangelical Or Missionary Or Academic Tool At Home, School, Bible Clubs, Sunday Schools, Church, Office And Other Fellowships

SUCCESSFUL CHRISTIANITY AND BASIC MINISTRIES
ISBN: 978-49874-6-0
A Collection Of Resource Materials That Precedes Christian Ministries And Basic Leadership Course Book

The first question is how Christianity is practiced even in a hostile environment. Next to that is the question about the potentials of Christians in spite of their apparent limitations. The other issues are connected to the successes, deliverance, callings, basic ministries of all Christians and evangelism. Various schools of thoughts have attempted these questions but many answers only portray Christianity as a form of religion instead of a way of life as specified by God. Some answers give room for compromise, hypocrisies, dogmas and denominational doctrines. The misconceptions about these areas of Christianity have brought about worldliness instead of righteousness and false achievements instead of fulfillment.

This book which contains six different subjects had been used to hold seminars at various levels, train ministers and Christian workers in Bible Schools and to equip the Church. It explains in simple terms the seemingly complex issues on practice of Christianity, Potentials, Deliverance, God's Kind Of Success, Evangelism and Basic Ministries of a Christian with Biblical principles, life transforming stories and illustrations.

CHRISTIAN MINISTRIES AND BASIC LEADERSHIP
ISBN: 978-36348-7-9 ISBN: 978-978-36348-7-9
A Collection Of Resource Materials That Follows Up Successful Christianity And Basic Ministries Course Book

As it is common to say that the hood does not make a monk, the dignified positions and bogus titles of many Christian leaders in modern days do not really make them Gospel Ministers.

This course book - a compilation of five resource materials on Missions And Outreach Ministries, Christian Communication Arts, Christian Leadership, Christian Education Methodology and Ministries Of Improvisations - aims at making every matured Christian an effective minister and leader at their respective homes, communities and nations. It teaches various ways Christians can communicate the word of God, meeting up to their responsibilities as ministers and leaders that reconcile people to God, edifying the Body Of Christ and reaching out to souls at the same time.

All of the resource materials are in use in Bible Schools like College Of Christian Education And Missions, in Churches and other ministries to raise Christian workers, Evangelists, Missionaries and other Ministers that serve at various levels and leadership capacities.

INSANITY OF HUMANITY
ISBN: 978-36348-6-0 ISBN: 978-978-36348-6-2
The Results Of Research Works Into Various Methods Of Brainwashing

Man is made to exercise his freewill. The mind of his own and the power to choose between right and wrong, good and evil, light and darkness is about to be washed away through brainwashing. The agents of control dubbed as Secret Government by John Todd (the top Illuninati defector) have put necessary machinery in place to ensure that all human beings are in conformity in their thinking and ways of life, trying to wipe away diversity, which makes each person unique.

This book attempts to shed light on how the techniques of mind control are applied through the use of propaganda, education, entertainments, drugs, religions, media and other means of communications. It is the result of research works, some of which are based on findings of various researchers and writers like Bugger Lugz, Edward Hunter, Hadley Cantril, Herbert Krugman, David L. Robb, Vaughan Bell, Juliana Gomez, Ryan Duffy Vice, Henry Makow, David Nicholls, Fritz Springmeire, Steven Hassan, Renate Thienel, Debra Pursell, Mary Pride and a host of others who are acknowledged in this book.

FOOTSTEPS IN THE MUD
ISBN: 978-36348-9-5 ISBN: 978-978-36348-9-3
The Drama Package Of Results Of Research Works That trace Global And Societal Vices To The Corrupt Or Lost Of Family Values

The 13-Episode drama book involves Bosede who learnt many wrong things from her parents' conduct and foul language. She was forced to marry Kola when she became pregnant. Using her mother's method to handle her father, she tried to subject Kola to her control. In the course of that, she made life terrible for him. Although her mother tried to warn her of the implications of maltreating her husband but Bosede has grown out of control. Consequently, while looking for peace, Kola was pushed out of the house. He made friends with some guys who taught him the unholy ways of life and influenced him to become a menace in the house.

Junior who was born at time the couple never proved to be responsible parents also learnt wrong things from them. He decided to follow his father's footsteps by taking alcohol when he was in primary school. As if that was not bad enough, he tried to teach other children in the school the madness in his home. A school teacher, however, was able to influence him and his mother by teaching them Christian morals. Even then, Junior was soon caught in the crossfire at home as his father tried to enlist him as a future member of a secret cult that posed as a social club.

NO MORE TEARS TO SHED
ISBN: 978-49874-3-0 ISBN: 978-978-74-3-1

Kidnappers took Tokunbo away from his grand parents in a city in Nigeria when he was a little boy. A nice woman found him in another town and gave him a false identity. She spoilt him with love, making him to grow into a rebellious teenager that was not appreciated anywhere. When Janet made him a Christian, however, life began to make sense to him until the day he was beaten to the point of death for the offence he knew nothing about. He left the town for the city which, unknown to him, held his true identity and the link to his parents in the United States. To find them was only a question of time.

THE UNROMANTIC LOVE BIRDS
ISBN: 978-4987-5-7 ISBN: 978-978-4974-5-5

And other short stories about love and marriages

They were very much in love right from their school days but when they got married and had children, romance became the game Charles' wife refused to play. No matter how much he tried to make her understand the unbearable condition her unromantic attitude has subjected him into, she would not change. Consequently, after enduring for so long, he was forced to look for the women that would make up for her weakness. He unofficially married a beautiful lady of insane jealousy. Though she was ready to give him what was missing in his marriage, it soon dawn on him that he has solved one big problem only to create a bigger one.

THE BATTLE OF THE CONQUERORS
ISBN: 978-49874-7-3 ISBN: ISBN: 978-978-49874-0-7-9

Wickedness takes over the land of Bondage from First Couple and subjects everybody into slavery without giving anybody the chance to be free. Love brings The Redeemer from Eternity and offers the slaves the chance to escape. Wickedness soon declares war and engages everyone in the battle. The Redeemer makes the redeemed people Conquerors by giving them the armour of war and Comforter but Wickedness cannot be undone. He has several thousands of years of experience in the war. So he is quick to recognize the weakness of the redeemed people who are ignorant of their strengths and advantages. Although the Conquerors fight like immutable giants, rescuing victims of war, many people suffer heavy casualties.

Since King Wickedness knows that a redeemed person is strong enough to chase one thousand of his warriors at a time, and two would put ten thousand into flight, he enlists as one of his warriors the people's deadliest enemy called Disunity.

Wickedness is able to strike the people by making them to fight with one another, turning what is supposed to be their best moments in the battle into tales of woes.

BLOODSHED IN CAMPUS
ISBN: 978-07350-3-8 ISBN: 978-978-07350-3-6

A poor widow tearfully warned her son, Richard, against joining the bad wagon when he got an admission into one of the Nigerian Universities. He resisted the membership of groups of students, including the Christian Fellowship until he had an encounter with a member of The Black Skulls - a deadly and ruthless secret cult on the campus.

Before Richard knew what he was up against, the head of The Black Skulls had arranged items for his initiation into the cult. While resisting being initiated, he ran to the Christian Fellowship for help. The leader of the Christian Fellowship dragged The President of Students' Union Government (S.U.G) into the conflict. With the involvement of the S.U.G President, another formidable cult called The Red Eyes felt obliged to team up against The Black Skulls. Then the campus turned into a battlefield and BLOODSHED became the order of the black day.

NETWORK BIBLE CLUB
YOUTH AND ADULT BOOK ONE
ISBN: 978 - 978- 49874-9-X ISBN: 978-978-49874-9-3

A collection of 26 life transforming stories, 26 poems, 26 hymn tuned songs and weekly Bible lessons

The issue of moral instructions in schools and at homes is

threatened with extinction. Consequently, so many youths are involved in prostitution, drug addictions, cultism, fraudulent practices, armed robberies and other crimes. Those who are supposed to be trained as leaders in various walks of life are the ones posing serious threats to many lives. Many parents who fail to add moral values to the upbringing of their children often times breed potential criminals under their roofs without knowing it. Apart from these, many other people negatively influence young ones through the media, music, publications, films, conduct and foul language; making them to lose their moral and family values.

This book one just like the rest of other volumes is an attempt to bring back moral instructions into schools and campuses through the use of stories, hymn tuned songs, poems, Bible lessons and class activities. It is designed to assist teachers and ministers in Secondary Schools, Bible Clubs, Churches and Campus Fellowships to teach people, especially youths the Word of God and serves as a school text book in subjects relating to literature, music and other creative works.

FOUNDATION BIBLE CLUB A-Z STORY BOOK
ISBN: 978-49874-2-2 ISBN: 978-978-49874-2-4
Volume 1 With 26 Stories, 26 Bible Lessons, 26 Rhymes And 26 Songs For Book For Young Minds

An adage says, "a man who builds a house without building his child builds what the child will later sell." Proverbs 22:6 says, "train up a child in the way he should go: and when he is old, he will not depart from it." This book is an attempt to assist parents and teachers to meet up to the challenges that befall them in carrying out this important function in the light of the moral decadence that is prevailing all over the world.

The first edition of the book was used by several thousands of teachers, ministers and parents in schools, Churches and homes to build the moral values of young ones. Apart from the stories, songs and Bible passages for the young ones to study, there is a seminar material that is based on the lecture which the author delivered to school proprietors, children ministers and Christian professionals in this volume.

RANSOM FOR LOVE
ISBN: 978-49874-8-1 ISBN: 978-978-4987-4-8-6

She accepted his marriage proposal without knowing the kind of person he was. She soon discovered that he was a mean and ruthless guy who was always ready to get whatever he wanted by all means even if he has to pay for it with the lives of others. She was in his bondage, especially when her parents who believed he was a generous and gentleman were on his side.

Because she considered the proposal to marry him as a marriage engagement with the devil incarnate, she decided that she would rather die than to share her life with him. Then out of the blues, this passionate gentleman sneaked into her life despite all she did to discourage him. She could not resist his love for her when he offered to set her free from the devil incarnate. Then the battle began – sooner than they anticipated.

THE WEIGHT OF DEATH
ISBN: 9978-36348-0-1 ISBN: 978-978-36348-0-0
(Story Of The Spirit Eyes Series)

PLAY ONE: HORROR IN THE FAMILY: Talimi probably did not envisage his death when he was trying to compel his son, Damola to succeed him in the occult Brotherhood. Other members of the secret cult were aware of the battle between them. So when Talimi died; his family, especially Damola who was a diehard Christian began to fall prey to the cult. Using all their powers and the spirit that posed as Talimi's ghost, the cult waged war against the family, tormenting and making them to be at loggerheads.

PLAY TWO: RITUAL KIDS' KIDNAPPERS: Victor and the rest of the members of the School Bible Club were taught that there are lots of evil people in this world but he did not understand why God allowed him to be among the children that were taken away from their parents. He soon understood that he was to be used by God to rescue other children who did not know that everyone that truly believes in Jesus has the power to overcome evil.

PLAY THREE: THE WEIGHT OF DEATH: Awoseun would not have known the real source of problems of mankind if his father had not given him the power to see demons tormenting the people in different ways. What he was yet to know, however, was the power of light over darkness. When he was caught in crossfire between these powers, he desperately sought for deliverance.

CALVARY ROCK RESOURCE BOOKLET EDITION ONE: CHILDREN OF GOD AND THE SLAVES
978-151-9370-631

The Quarterly Missionary Booklets That Are Designed To Teach Children, Youths And Adults In Schools, Fellowships, Churches, At Homes, Office And Other Places.

Although all the various volumes of this booklet can be used independently of other books but it is recommended that it should be used as part of supplementary materials to make up for Foundation and Network Bible Club Story Books for both children and adults in School, Church, Campus, Office and other Fellowships.

Each of the volume is rich with quarterly Bible lessons, stories, drama, songs, seminar, tract materials and a host of other things that can be used to edify, educate, entertains and evangelize every category of people, ranging from children to elderly persons.

Every volume is designed to equip school teachers, ministers in Churches or campus or office fellowships and other people who wish to work with the Lord.

All These And Other Books Are Distributed Worldwide And Published By The Publishing House Of Calvary Rock Resources

*Ikenne-Remo, Nigeria
*Manchester, United Kingdom
*New York, United States

www.calvaryrock.org

www.ingramcontent.com/pod-product-compliance
Lightning Source LLC
Chambersburg PA
CBHW020012050426
42450CB00005B/433